Otto
von Bismarck

PROBLEMS IN EUROPEAN CIVILIZATION

Under the editorial direction of
John Ratté
Amherst College

Otto von Bismarck

A Historical Assessment

Second Edition

Edited and with an introduction by

Theodore S. Hamerow
University of Wisconsin

D. C. HEATH AND COMPANY
Lexington, Massachusetts Toronto

CONTENTS

IV ARBITER OF EUROPE

V THE IRON CHANCELLOR

VI THE BISMARCKIAN LEGACY

INTRODUCTION

The theory that history is determined by the great men of an age has long been out of fashion. Even while Thomas Carlyle was delivering his brilliant lectures *On Heroes, Hero Worship and the Heroic in History* more than a hundred years ago, there were those in the audience who refused to be swayed by his eloquence. And the general trend of historical thinking since those days has been away from the doctrine of the omnipotent genius. Some of us believe that the destiny of our world is being shaped by ideals like democracy, nationalism, the classless society, or the greatest happiness of the greatest number. Others, that the distribution of material resources and rewards forms the essential character of a civilization. There are those who feel that the ultimate arbiter of human affairs is armed might, the ability to create and use nuclear bombs, robot aircraft, space satellites, nerve gases. A few will even maintain that we are all ultimately in the grip of those irrational and subconscious forces which Sigmund Freud discovered deep in man's psyche. But believers in the heroic determination of history are few and far between.

Yet in a sense we covertly accept what we publicly deny. Men may insist on the primacy of ideology in affairs of state, or on the importance of economic relationships, or on the arbitrament of arms, or on the might of the libido. But in practice they behave as if it made a great deal of difference whether Johnson or Nixon, de Gaulle or Pompidou, Adenauer or Brandt, Brezhnev or Mao Tse-tung decides policy. Apparently personalities are not unimportant after all. What is more, on reflection we would probably have to concede that in times of crisis the role of the individual becomes particularly significant. Would the Union have been preserved, if James Buchanan rather than Abraham Lincoln had been inaugurated as president of the United States in the spring of 1861? Could a disorganized faction of doctrinaire radicals have seized power in Russia in 1917, if Lenin had never taken that trip across Germany in a sealed train? How would the people of England have responded in 1940, if Neville Chamberlain or Lord Halifax had demanded of them blood, sweat, and tears? Willy-nilly, we are forced into a semi-Carlylean position. There is a group of political leaders—consider Napoleon, Cavour, Lincoln, Lenin, Churchill—who exercised a profound political influence on the course of events at some crucial point in history. In a very important respect they are the makers of the world in which we live.

Otto von Bismarck belongs in this company. And yet the significance of the part which he played in public affairs remains a subject of bitter dispute more than seventy years after his death. His fellows in the pantheon of statesmen have been consigned to their niches, their strengths and weaknesses engraved in marble for all time. They no longer arouse passion; they are no longer controversial. They have ceased to be flesh and blood; they are now tradition. Today the English are willing to admit that Napoleon was not the incarnation of Satan after all, while the French do not insist that he was the greatest hero since Alexander. Lincoln has become a deity of popular democracy in America; we all see him as he sits in that magnificent sculpture by Daniel Chester French, gazing down upon the world with an inexhaustible compassion. Churchill became apotheosized during his own lifetime, like some Roman emperor of the dying ancient world. No one disputes that Hitler was a man of infinite evil. Even Lenin embalmed in the Kremlin has become a saint to dedicated communists, a devil to violent reactionaries, and a leader of great gifts serving questionable ends to those in between.

But Bismarck is a law unto himself. The same controversies which raged around the Iron Chancellor while he was alive continue to trouble his eternal rest. He has been portrayed as both the destroyer of liberty and a compromiser with liberalism. His wars of unification are to some a work of political duplicity, to others an act of historic justice. There are those who see in his diplomacy an attempt to maintain German hegemony; others who consider it proof of his wish to preserve the old Europe. His efforts to crush Catholicism and socialism have been explained as the folly of a ruthless authoritarian, or as the struggle of a wise statesman to subdue the forces of national disruption. The clash of opposing interpretations goes on.

The issues posed by Bismarck's statecraft cannot be reduced to a simple formulation. Was he good or bad, a realist or an idealist? Was he a conservative of the old school or a totalitarian forerunner of National Socialism? Was he a "good European" or an advocate of *Deutschland über alles*? These questions are too shallow, too naive to lead to answers which can contribute significantly to our comprehension. The dimensions of the problem are too great to be measured in such antonymous juxtapositions as "innocent or guilty," "progressive or reactionary," "Christian or Machiavellian." It can even be argued that there really is no such thing as a Bismarck problem, that there are rather several Bismarcks and several problems. A statesman whose career extended over thirty years, who helped maintain royal prerogative against parliamentary claims, who successfully asserted Prussia's demand for power in the face of Austrian opposition, who encompassed the fall of one empire in France and established another in Germany, who waged war against the Vatican as well as against Marxism, who directed the diplomatic fortunes of a continent, such a statesman cannot be categorized under any single rubric. To understand the rich complexity of his achievement we must examine it in a variety of contexts and from several points of view.

This book, therefore, begins with a consideration of those personal qualities and private experiences which helped transform a fire-eating reactionary aristocrat into a discerning and imaginative diplomat. The landed noblemen of Prussia among whom Bismarck grew up were a social class distinguished for neither subtlety nor judgment. Yet the Junker of Schönhausen somehow managed to overcome the limitations imposed by his background. When he first entered politics in his thirties as a delegate to the United Diet of 1847, he was an uncompromising enemy of parliamentary government. Twenty years later he became the author of a constitution which gave the suffrage to every adult male, at a time when even in England most men still could not vote. During the revolution of 1848 he worked tirelessly to frustrate liberal plans for the unification of Germany. On January 18, 1871, he stood proudly in the Hall of Mirrors at Versailles, while the German Empire which he had helped create was being proclaimed. At the time of the Austro-Prussian conflict of 1850 he was all for moderation and monarchical solidarity. By 1859 he had become so violently opposed to the diplomacy of the Hofburg that the authorities in Berlin thought it best to send him into genteel exile in the embassy at St. Petersburg. The conservative friends of his youth, who could still remember him as an ultra of the ultras, observed his change of heart first with surprise, then dismay, and finally resentment, until they broke with him at the moment of his greatest triumph. But Bismarck went on maturing in his view of the world long after most men harden in the rigid mold of everyday life.

Why? How could the harsh, stubborn soil of the Prussian latifundia produce a statesman of such subtlety and perception? Here is the question which has fascinated all of his biographers. The ultimate mystery of Bismarck's personality remains unsolved; it is probably insoluble. But there are partial answers which can enlarge our understanding of the man. Some writers have seen in him above all a country squire of genius, attached to the soil, close to nature, distrustful of the big city with its disintegrating effect on human loyalty. Hence his devotion to the traditions of the state; hence his criticism of the liberal addiction to experiment and innovation. Others have focused on the formative intellectual experiences of his youth: on the tendency toward philosophic skepticism; on the romanticist strain in him; above all, on the Pietistic ethic of his Pomeranian friends. It is also clear that the years Bismarck spent in Frankfurt as Prussian representative at the Diet of the German Confederation were a turning point. He was forced to the conclusion that some form of German unification was inevitable, and that it ought to be *kleindeutsch* in form, realized under Hohenzollern auspices to the exclusion of Austrian influence. Finally, the art of biography in the twentieth century cannot escape the influence of the Freudian technique and vocabulary. There are those who try to understand the grown statesman by analyzing his childhood experiences, his relationship to his parents, the emotional atmosphere of the paternal home, his youthful associations with men and women. These diverse interpretations of Bismarck as a man are not mutually inconsistent. They differ in emphasis and point of view, but they are complementary rather than exclusive. If they do not resolve the problem, they at least define and clarify it.

While Bismarck the man interests us from the day of his birth or perhaps even one or two generations before that, Bismarck the statesman becomes important only with his appointmont as primo minister of Prussia in 1862. He came to power at a critical moment. For the third time in fifty years the liberals were trying to introduce parliamentary rule in the Hohenzollern monarchy. They had failed once after 1815, when a political reaction followed the exalted mood of the War of Liberation. They had failed again after 1848, when royalist armies crushed the bright hopes of the revolution. Now they were once more challenging the tradition of monarchical absolutism. The immediate issue in the constitutional conflict was army reform, but on its outcome depended the future of representative government in Germany. If the legislature won the right to control the armed forces through the power of the purse, it could go on to assert its authority over all other functions of government as well. The experience of Great Britain would then be repeated in Central Europe.

But Bismarck succeeded in taming parliament. For four long years he governed in defiance of the chamber and in violation of the constitution, until he finally forced the opposition to accept a settlement on his terms. By defeating Austria in the Seven Weeks' War and consolidating all of Germany north of the Main River, he was able to offer the parliamentarians something which was even more precious to them than their parliamentarianism, a united national state. It was an offer they could not resist. By a vote of 230 to 75 the legislature adopted a bill of indemnity legalizing all the transgressions for which it had repeatedly condemned the prime minister. The best hope of German liberalism failed, and the results of that historic failure continue to be felt a hundred years later.

No aspect of Bismarck's statecraft has been the subject of as much controversy as his role in undermining parliamentary institutions in Germany. His other accomplishments can be regarded with greater equanimity, since they no longer affect us in any immediate way. The empire which he built did not survive him by more than twenty years. His complicated system of diplomatic alliances and alignments began to fall apart almost on the day of his dismissal in

1890. His war against Catholics and Marxists recalls King Canute ordering the rising tide of the Thames to go back. But the corruption of liberalism, that is a different story. It leads directly to the personal rule of William II, to the dictatorship of the high command during the First World War, to the tragedy of the Weimar Republic, to the horror of the Third Reich. It summons us irresistibly to take sides. During his lifetime Bismarck was portrayed by many writers as the great compromiser who sought to maintain a healthy balance between monarchical authority and popular democracy. After all, while he may not have approved of parliamentarian doctrines, neither did he agree with the reactionaries who were urging him to re-establish royal absolutism. In the twentieth century, however, he ceased to be the voice of sweet reasonableness. After the fall of the German Empire in 1918 his partisans and critics alike tended to become more drastic. Those who were out of sympathy with democratic institutions invoked his name to prove that only a heroic leader could save their nation from the self-seeking politicians. And those who deplored the growth of totalitarianism in Central Europe attacked his achievement, partly because it led to the seduction of the liberals, partly because it persuaded the liberals to let themselves be seduced. The differences of opinion remain unresolved.

The diplomatic means which Bismarck used to achieve the unification of Germany are controversial as well, for no sharp distinction can be drawn between his domestic and foreign policies. From the beginning he planned to exploit success in the national struggle in order to prevail in the constitutional conflict. Shortly after his appointment as prime minister he outlined his program of action with frightening candor: "The great questions of the time are not decided by speeches and majority resolutions—that was the big mistake of 1848 and 1849—but by iron and blood." Armed force was for him always an essential element in the relations among governments; he never hesitated to use it where the stakes were high enough. And what stakes could be higher than the establishment of a united German state under the hegemony of Prussia? Not only would patriotic aspirations be realized through the leadership of the Hohenzollerns rather than the Habsburgs, but the clamor for parliamentary government would be stilled by a great national triumph won under monarchical authority. Domestic, national, and international issues of the greatest import were involved in the diplomatic game of the 1860s which Bismarck played with such consummate skill.

First he induced the Austrians to join him in a brief and successful war against Denmark for the provinces of Schleswig and Holstein. Then he saw to it that no agreement was reached with Vienna regarding the disposition of the spoils of victory. He still had some hope that the Hofburg could be bribed or frightened into agreeing to Prussian predominance in northern Germany. But when the imperial cabinet refused to back down, he decided to risk all in the Seven Weeks' War. Luck was with him. Prussian arms won a swift victory at Sadowa (Königgrätz) which enabled him to form the North German Confederation. Overnight the hated reactionary prime minister became a national demigod. The patriots walked on clouds, the liberals swallowed their scruples, the particularists were intimidated, the Austrians sulked. Only France openly expressed alarm at the establishment on her eastern frontier of a united Germany which her statesmen had opposed for more than three centuries. But Napoleon III was no match for Bismarck. The Franco-Prussian War led to the overthrow of the Bonaparte dynasty and to the proclamation of the empire of the Hohenzollerns. While the siege guns were booming around cold, starving Paris, the work of German unification was completed on January 18, 1871, at Prussian headquarters in Versailles.

How should this work be assessed? Those who lived in the state which Bismarck created usually found little fault with it. It brought them prosperity, respect, strength, and a sense of accomplishment. After its collapse, however, historians began to wonder about the soundness of the foundation on which it had rested. The German Empire lasted forty-seven years. It was followed by the Weimar Republic, which collapsed within fifteen years. Then came the Third Reich, destroyed twelve years later at the cost of a terrible world conflict. Out of its ruins emerged a diminished and divided people living in the shadow of foreign invasion. Here is a disheartening history of almost a hundred years of disappointed hopes, of wasted efforts, of wars, revolutions, depressions, tyrannies. Can it be that the source of the trouble lies in the way in which a nation was welded out of the diverse lands of Central Europe?

There are those who think so. To begin with, for some Austrians the verdict of 1866 has been hard to accept. They see in it the tragic

end of a historic association of a thousand years between their state
and the rest of the Germanic commonwealth, for it left them isolated
in a Slavic sea which was eventually bound to overwhelm them. They
are the latter-day advocates of the *grossdeutsch* idea, the idea that
Germany should be constituted with the participation and under the
leadership of Austria. Then there are the French scholars to whom
the achievement of a united German state is inextricably bound up
with the loss of Alsace and Lorraine. Their dislike of the eternal
Boche was probably greatest around the time of the First World War.
But even after their country regained the lost provinces, they
managed to restrain their admiration of Prussian statesmanship. Yet
Bismarck is not without his defenders. They contend that in an age
of rampant nationalism the unification of Germany was a historic
necessity which could not be realized except through blood and
iron. As for the Franco-Prussian War, the jingoes in Paris were as
vociferous as those in Berlin. If Napoleon III lost his crown, he had
only his own folly to blame.

The fall of the Second French Empire meant a diplomatic revolution in Europe. For the next half century Germany was the mightiest
state on the Continent, and during the first twenty years of that
period Bismarck was at the helm. His remarkable talents as a statesman were now displayed on a stage greater than that provided by
the constitutional conflict in Prussia or even by the long duel with
Austria. He had become in effect the arbiter of Europe. How did he
use the great power which was at his disposal? Here is the one point
in the lifework of the Iron Chancellor on which there is a high degree
of agreement. As a practitioner of the art of diplomacy he is without
a peer. His grasp of detail, his insight into motive, his ability to
sense the limitations as well as opportunities inherent in each new
international development, his tireless search for alternative solutions
to every major political problem, his willingness to retreat at the
precise moment when risks begin to outweigh advantages, they all
bespeak the master craftsman. There can simply be no gainsaying
the technical virtuosity of the man.

Yet virtuosity in a statesman is not without its dangers. The very
magnitude of the successes which Bismarck enjoyed tended to make
him appear inimitable and to transform his diplomacy into an occult

science no one but he could master. William I, a ruler not easily impressed, once exclaimed to his prime minister: "You seem to me at times to be like a rider who juggles on horseback with five balls, never letting one fall." The spell which the wizard of the Wilhelmstrasse cast over his contemporaries was irresistible. What he bequeathed to his country, however, was a legend rather than a vital political creed. Only Bismarck could practice Bismarckian statecraft. Once he fell, his successors found themselves enmeshed in international complications which they had never been taught to understand. For he had guarded the secrets of his trade jealously, like some statesman of the age of absolutism, like Mazarin or Kaunitz. But the nineteenth century was a dangerous time for personal diplomacy. The growing complexity of international relations arising out of the advance of technology, the rise of nationalism, and the movement to democracy called for a system of leadership independent of any personality however brilliant. Because he failed to provide that leadership, the founder of the German Empire must share responsibility for the collapse of his creation.

Most historians, however, have been too concerned with the immediate achievements of Bismarck's diplomacy to speculate about its ultimate implications. Those achievements are admittedly impressive. There is agreement, first of all, that once Germany was united, the Iron Chancellor became a tireless defender of peace in Europe. Not that he was in any sense a pacifist; he was always ready to use armed force to achieve his ends. Had he not deliberately provoked three important wars between 1864 and 1870? But he had never accepted the doctrine of boundless expansion, he had never succumbed to the temptation of cheap conquest. The German Empire was for him a "saturated" state, a state which had succeeded in satisfying all of its legitimate territorial aspirations. It had nothing to gain and everything to lose from a major European conflict. That intricate web of alliances and alignments which he spun with such painstaking care had as its object the maintenance of the status quo. But the achievement of this object was contingent on the isolation of France, the only major power whose vital national interests could not be satisfied without a war. Some writers have emphasized the pacific aspect of Bismarck's policy, others the anti-French aspect.

Actually, the two were opposite sides of a single coin, different but inseparable. They were both essential to the equilibrium which the *Pax Teutonica* maintained in Europe for twenty years.

Bismarck the diplomat has won the admiration of many, the respect of all. Bismarck the prime minister of a constitutional state invites criticism. He was too much the Prussian Junker to understand fully the profound political changes taking place about him during the later years of his life. In democracy he saw only the lust for power of unscrupulous politicians. Socialism was worse still; it meant the alienation of the urban masses from throne and altar, the most cherished institutions of society. As for the Roman Catholic Church, it was a foreign establishment propagating unpatriotic doctrines. Its power had to be crushed. The Iron Chancellor threw himself with all his boundless energy into the struggle against those forces which seemed to threaten the values he had spent his life upholding. First there was the *Kulturkampf*, the war against papal influence, which only served to fortify the adherents of the Clerical Center Party. It was followed by an even more ruthless campaign against socialism with the same disappointing results. The Social Democratic Party was driven underground, but it managed to survive and even increase in strength. Bismarck could still act with daring and imagination. During the 1880s he broke with the prevalent creed of laissez-faire individualism, introducing the first comprehensive system of social legislation in the world. But insurance of the industrial worker against sickness, accident, and old age failed to exorcise the specter of Marxism. In the end the chancellor was forced to contemplate a *coup d'état* leading to a fundamental alteration of the state which he himself had founded.

He never put this plan into effect. The same royal authority which he had defended so brilliantly throughout his career was now used to encompass his downfall. The young William II who came to the throne in 1888 was too impetuous and too ambitious to accept the tutelage of any man. The contest between emperor and chancellor could have only one outcome. The aging giant was unceremoniously forced into retirement, where he continued to grumble his displeasure with the course followed by the new masters of Germany. He lived long enough to see the beginning disintegration of his lifework.

But that work was probably doomed in any event. Bismarck had succeeded in discrediting representative institutions and in weakening the party system. He never encouraged independence in those around him, refusing to tolerate anyone whose talents might possibly compete with his own. Especially in his later years he became insufferably domineering, so that his fall was greeted by many of those who knew him best with a deep sigh of relief. He had never recognized that an enduring political system cannot be the achievement of any one man, whatever his strength or determination. He was admittedly no doctrinaire, no phrasemonger. He always stood head and shoulders above the narrow-minded landed aristocrats from whom he had sprung. But with all his intellectual suppleness and perception he never freed himself completely from the illusion that the old can be preserved indefinitely if it is only made to look like new. History has demonstrated the impossibility of his dream, but through sheer political wizardry he came as close to realizing it as any statesman can approach the impossible.

What is then the Bismarckian legacy to the twentieth century? As with everything else about the Iron Chancellor, historians differ. But never has there been as much criticism of his accomplishment as today. The ultimate collapse of everything for which he worked was bound to raise doubts about his methods and objectives. His exaltation of the policy of blood and iron encouraged among his countrymen a worship of power at the expense of justice. His rejection of a federalist solution of the political problems confronting Central Europe led to growing national tension and to an irreconcilable conflict between Slav and Teuton. Austria ceased to play her traditional role as organizer and civilizer of her neighbors to the east and south. Deprived of her historic mission, she atrophied and disintegrated. As for Germany, she too was unable to develop a healthy existence within the framework provided by the Hohenzollern empire. The golden memories of Sadowa and Sedan have long been extinguished by lost world wars, disastrous inflations, territorial losses, population expulsions, concentration camps, gas chambers. Perhaps the entire work of unification was built on a false foundation. Bismarck's critics also point to his failure to train his nation in the art of self-government. The frailty of democratic institutions in Germany contributed to totalitarianism, to world conflict, and to the devastation of a continent. The world today is in a sense still paying for the mistakes of the 1860s.

But the Iron Chancellor has his admirers as well. Nor can they be dismissed as mere tub-thumping chauvinists repeating the perennial slogans of professional patriotism. Many of them are scholars of the first rank who see in Bismarck precisely those qualities of moderation and reasonableness which the statesmanship of our own day needs so desperately. At no time did he preach doctrines of racial superiority or unlimited conquest. He always believed in a balance of power resting upon the secure existence of several major states. Germany was to have a primary, but not a preponderant position in the councils of Europe. He consistently rejected all claims to totalitarian power on the part of government, and even bureaucratic arbitrariness was a weapon which he used sparingly. He liked to play the bluff Junker, strutting in military uniform and indulging in such rodomontade as: "We Germans fear God and nothing else in the world." Actually, he was always careful to respect the vital interests of other nations, unless they conflicted directly with those of his own. Even his treatment of political opponents revealed a restraint which disappointed the extremists in his camp. The Progressives, the Conservatives, the Centrists, the Socialists, the Poles, they all attacked him repeatedly in parliament and press. But he never proposed to deal with them in the time-honored fashion of dictators by putting them up against a wall and ordering the firing squad to shoot. The barbarities of National Socialism would no doubt have horrified him. Friedrich Meinecke recounts that a Danish friend admitted to him during the Third Reich: "You know I cannot love Bismarck, but now I must say: Bismarck belongs to *our* world."

It is clear that the time for a definitive assessment of the Iron Chancellor has not arrived. It may never come. For each successive generation seems to find a new meaning in his career. As our experiences change us, so we change our interpretation of the experiences of others. We are always writing history anew. The outcome of the First World War forces us to rethink the Franco-Prussian War. The fact that democracy failed in Germany in 1933 suggests a new evaluation of the constitutional conflict in Prussia in 1862–1866. The New Deal calls to mind the social legislation of the 1880s. The formation of NATO invites us to study once again the Triple Alliance. Yet the inescapable conclusion that historical understanding will be different tomorrow from what it is today, just as today it is different from what it was yesterday, should not lead us to a paralyzing relativism. We have the duty to sit in judgment on the past in the light of our standard of right and wrong. But in order to judge fairly we must familiarize ourselves with the facts of the case, we must weigh with care the pros and cons. In the case of Bismarck the verdict is particularly difficult. Like the spirit of Caesar, his ghost walks abroad among us, raising questions which are as pertinent to our own time as to his. To answer them we must examine our own attitudes toward the crucial beliefs and institutions of society. We must ponder the nature of political democracy, national sovereignty, military might, diplomatic hegemony, economic justice. In the search for a solution of the Bismarckian enigma we will of necessity achieve a deeper understanding of the problems facing us in the critical times in which we live.

Conflict of Opinion

He was not striving for world-dominion nor for boundless power, but for the means to secure and strengthen his Prussian Fatherland. So much acquisition of power and of territory as was necessary for this he laid hold of with iron grasp—so much and no more. The intoxication of victory never disordered his judgment, nor got the mastery over his fixed principles of moderation.

HEINRICH VON SYBEL

. . . that extraordinary man, the craftiest of foxes, the boldest of lions, who had the art of fascinating and of terrifying, of making of truth itself an instrument of falsehood; to whom gratitude, forgiveness of injuries, and respect for the vanquished were as entirely unknown as all other noble sentiments save that of devotion to his country's ambition; who deemed legitimate everything that contributes to success and who, by his contempt for the importunities of morality, dazzled the imagination of mankind.

ÉMILE OLLIVIER

The nation did not recognize her savior, would, in fact, willingly have crucified him or burned him alive. He had to save his country as he once saved a groom from drowning, by gripping it by the throat. When he had won and the work was practically over, then they cheered and lauded him to the skies. But what was the value of such belated converts? From the vast majority of the nation there never came a spark of understanding for the statesman who gave them what they wanted but had been incapable of obtaining themselves.

JOHANNES HALLER

We may criticize Bismarck for many good reasons, for paving the way to some fatal trends of our days, but while doing so we cannot very well overlook the fundamental fact that Hitler, in almost every respect, did precisely what the founder of the Reich had refused to do. Many of those who were under the heel inside or outside Germany, had an appreciation of this fact. And thus the word of the Danish historian may be taken up once more as a summary which draws the essential frontier line: Bismarck certainly "belonged to our world," that is, to the anti-Hitlerian world.

HANS ROTHFELS

In his *Thoughts and Recollections* he declares that his aim was to earn the confidence of lesser and greater powers by a peaceful, just, honest and conciliatory policy. It almost sounds like a belated palliation of his essentially Machiavellian statesmanship. Yet the further we carry our researches, the clearer is the evidence that he was only putting into words the fundamental principle of his actions.

                                                                ERICH BRANDENBURG

One must regard Bismarck as a borderline case. He still had in mind to some extent the conception of a synthesis of power and culture as it was understood by the leaders of the movement for German unity. These leaders themselves, with Treitschke at their head, originally were seriously offended by Bismarck's first steps in the period of the constitutional conflict, but became his defenders and admirers as a consequence of the war of 1866. The result was that in the synthesis of power and culture, of the things of the state and the things of the spirit, the preponderance slowly but steadily shifted further over to the side of power and its domain.

                                                                FRIEDRICH MEINECKE

His had been a great career, beginning with three wars in eight years and ending with a period of twenty years during which he worked for the peace of Europe, despite countless opportunities to embark on further enterprises with more than an even chance of success. No other statesman of his standing had ever before shown the same great moderation and sound political sense of the possible and the desirable.

                                                                WILLIAM L. LANGER

He made shift with the old means and the old purposes. This had never before led to enduring order; now the passions were all aroused as well. Bismarck took part in this release from control. He believed that he could utilize the new impulsion to be found in the crowd for the power of his state, and at the same time limit it by a rational system called reason of state. He did not come to a realization that in a world of such confusions there are tasks which go far beyond the state, and that it was becoming extremely necessary to bring the state back to its original purpose, to help establish the good, the right, the higher order. His position remained that the statesman's task consisted in nothing more than development of the state.

                                                                FRANZ SCHNABEL

I THE MAKING OF A STATESMAN

Erich Marcks

A COUNTRY SQUIRE

*More than sixty years ago the eminent German scholar Erich Marcks pub-
lished the first volume of what promised to become the classic life of the
Iron Chancellor. But at the time of his death in 1938 the next part of the
biography had still not appeared. Perhaps the task was too great for even
his considerable talents. What we have is only a fragment, a fragment
suggesting the heroic proportions of the unfinished design. In its grand
scope and meticulous detail it reveals the admiration of the biographer for
his subject. Marcks emphasizes in the following selection the importance of
Bismarck's experiences as a landed aristocrat.*

During those years he was a farmer pure and simple. He was active
on various commissions of the Regenwald Agricultural Association
in 1842, 1844, and 1845, was once recommended by it for a royal
prize, borrowed from it (1843) many books and periodicals on agriculture and economics. A neighbor of Bismarck later told von
Keudell about his study of topography in maps and books, and about
his amazing knowledge of the soil and value of estates in Pomerania,
the Mark, and the Magdeburg region. But above all, letters to various
members of his family reflect again and again his physical and
spiritual dedication to farming. They tell about his activities, about
the weather, about crop conditions, about horses and laborers,
about frosts, diseases, natural calamities and prices, about his own
estate and the situation of others, and about his observations on
economic conditions abroad. A part of his account books has been
preserved. There are long sections in his own handwriting, the entries
arranged by date, neatly and carefully classified under various categories of receipts and expenditures, balanced for each month, the
vertical letters pressed close together. Among the receipts those
from wool are most important, but on one occasion there is also
mention of a small sum won in gambling. The expenditures column
includes large amounts and small, business outlays and personal
expenses: machinery, seed, wages, insurance, taxes and county

From Erich Marcks, *Bismarck: Eine Biographie, 1815–1851* (Stuttgart, 1951), pp. 150–
155. Reprinted by permission of Deutsche Verlags-Anstalt. Translated by Theodore S.
Hamerow and William W. Beyer.

fees, and then the costs of travel, innkeeper's bills, gratuities, modest gambling debts, but also an entry "50 taler for the victims of the fire in Trieglaff" (1845). Bismarck borrowed money and paid it back to businessmen, friends, and relatives, and in turn helped the latter out. His published letters have told us much about his business affairs; for example, about his unexpected trouble with taxes during his trip to France in 1842, when his father and brother proved very helpful. These financial difficulties never ceased entirely, not even at Schönhausen. Yet there can be no doubt that his work was highly profitable. He wrote in 1884 to one of his friends from the university days at Göttingen, affecting the bantering tone of a student: "For five years I have lived alone in the country and devoted myself with some success to the enlargement of my school allowance." The figures with which he explained to his fiancée (February 13, 1847) the increase in value of his three estates speak for themselves: what he had vainly tried to sell for 150,000 taler in 1838 was now valued at 200,000, and even that estimate was too low.

Did this work also give him the freedom and the joy of creativity which he had expected when he wrote to Countess Bismarck-Bohlen at the time of his change of occupation? "I have recovered through experience from illusions about the rustic happiness of an inveterate farmer, with double-entry bookkeeping and the study of chemistry," he told his fiancée nine years later. But in the meantime he had devoted himself to his work and been profoundly influenced by it. In spite of his growing complaints, he was a dedicated farmer and in a sense remained one all his life. It is not only the letters to his family reporting his adjustment to living in Schönhausen which prove this point. Even from Versailles he kept watch over the estate at Varzin with surprising solicitude, composing long written instructions as if there were no war to wage and no German Empire to build.

He came to identify himself with his environment as never before. He worked in the garden with great fondness. How difficult was it for him in 1847 to part from his "plants and lawns, from the white bridges and benches." He had planned to build a new house. He regarded Kniephof with all of the nobleman's love for land, a love which he then transferred to Schönhausen; he regarded it with all the tenderness of his childhood memories. He himself had felt during those years the patriarchal affection which he later praised in his article of 1848. His relationship to the laborers who had dutifully served his father for so long was full of mutual trust. In a letter to his fiancée he describes their tearful farewells and their fears that the future manager of the estate might prove unkind. But he was not the only witness on this point. In 1899 Reinhold von Thadden, the son of Bismarck's neighbors in Trieglaff, wrote his recollections of the great man, recollections which tell us much about those youthful years. He too remembered how Bismarck admired the cheerful friendliness of Senfft-Pilsach toward his workers, and how his own dealings with those beneath him were exemplary, completely free of any haughtiness. According to his friend Moritz von Blanckenburg, Bismarck spoke to each of his servants as if to a member of his own circle of acquaintances. In January 1844 Blanckenburg himself wrote to him in the course of a chatty, friendly letter:

> *Otto, are you not a kind person . . . are you not a master with a warm heart for your servants, a master who is just to all and gives each his due . . . ? We both have the same calling on earth, and I would be very pleased, if I could get along with the people who work for me as well as is commonly said about you.*

Only in those years apparently did he become entirely fluent in Low German. And only then did he get to know the country and its people, by dealing with them directly. Years later at the dinner table he enjoyed describing Pomeranian types, Jews, noblemen. He relied on his sympathy and familiarity with the peasants, with their way of thinking and feeling, with their needs and problems, in many of the great speeches which he delivered as chancellor in support of his tax and tariff policies. The von Thaddens learned in 1844 with pleasant surprise how well he could deal with rustics, when he represented them after a destructive fire in negotiations with the peasants of Trieglaff. And only in those years did he acquire that vast knowledge of the soil and of all things pertaining to it with which he was still able to astonish city people in his eighties. Here was a land of wide horizons, resembling the region where his ancestors had lived. . . . It was a land which rewarded only patient effort, a land which tended to encourage sobriety. He learned to observe it in detail in the life of the smallest creature in his park, as well as on a large scale on his rolling fields and meadows. He directed his supervising glance at daily growth and development. Like every countryman he came to feel the great human dependence on the powers of nature, on weather, on rain, on frost, on pestilence. As owner of his land he no doubt experienced what the greatest rustic poet of our people has praised as the unobtrusive yet urgent lesson of agriculture: the repose which devoutly anticipates the germination and development of the bud, the moderation which must admit every day that trees do not grow as high as the sky, the assurance that crops can be harvested only "when the color and the weight of the fruit tell that the time has come." He also learned to be observant, matter-of-fact, realistic; a limited occupation taught him to master a well-defined field of endeavor and its problems. He had become a huntsman early in life, and now he pursued the sport more than ever. The hunt trained him to scout, to reconnoiter, to lie in wait, to watch, and then act quickly and effectively. He rode far and wide on his loyal Caleb through the Pomeranian countryside, "over many a mile, happy and sad, angry and calm, past moors and fields, past lakes and houses and people." Even as an old man he enjoyed rides and trips, gazing about him and trying to see all. A quarter of a century later he could still surprise Reinhold Thadden with the infallible accuracy of his recollections about the boundaries of parishes and the points of the compass.

The impressions of those long years in the country greatly affected the policies and decisions of his later life. It has long been noted that in the extraordinary richness of his language the most characteristic, novel, and perceptive expressions are always derived from the country, from houses and roofs and barrels and pots, from riding and travel, from streets and bridges, from farming with all its skills and sorrows, from horse trading, from the hunt. Soil, animals and plants, weather and heat and disease provided him with insight and comparison. The proverbial, the popular, the natural grew on him, rose to his lips. Even bills of exchange and mortgages were familiar to him and became part of his vocabulary. Everything was experienced reality. "By the time of the next partridge hunt I'll be married," he announces laconically to his brother in April 1847.

All this was not new in his character. His language had from the beginning suggested rural, aristocratic primitiveness and tradition.

He knew as early as 1838 what drew him so passionately to the country. But the full realization must have come later; only later was his life filled with it. Above all, only later did he become master of his estate, and that was what he had always desired most of all. He could now command his land and his people; he no longer needed to obey. As lord of the manor he kept the record in his large, firm script whenever the mayor, the preacher, or the schoolmaster from Jarchelin squabbled about fees. He exercised police power. Although a free member of the governing class, he soon subordinated himself more and more to the aristocratic government of the country. Still, he had to make his decisions independently, and he led a lonely life on his estate, like many of his class. Yet he was separated from the others by a wide gulf. Even this loneliness of which he was to complain so often with the passage of time belongs to the formative forces of this period of his life, and is related to his freedom and pride. The oak grows broadest and strongest when it grows alone. He knew that very well. On November 3, 1870, he spoke at Versailles about the difference between the city and the country. Because of its direct contact with nature, the countryside makes people more practical. The big city makes them too clever. It creates mass opinions out of thin air, out of rumors and counterrumors, without any basis in fact. It breeds unshakable mass superstitions, which spin a web around people and soon appear to them duties and obligations: "Where so many men live close together, individual characteristics disappear easily, they melt together." It does not matter whether in these chatty observations Count Bismarck was being fair to the individualism which the city and its culture develop, the modern, democratic individualism of whose unattractive side he spoke. The point is that he revealed a deep-seated feeling which he had acquired in the country. He believed in a differently conceived, unrefined, autocratic individualism; he believed in an aristocratic personality rooted in the soil, completely self-reliant, acting freely and generously, a personality growing out of the past and growing into every new epoch, nourished by ancient tradition, and yet an expression of eternally youthful individualistic forces. This is the personality which ripened in him during his years in Pomerania, which intermingled with the great fullness of his most intimate qualities. This is the personality which

strengthened and broadened and grew to those heights to which it
was one day triumphantly to exalt a people.

Hajo Holborn
FORMATIVE INTELLECTUAL EXPERIENCES

*Hajo Holborn belonged to the generation of German scholars which reached
maturity under the Weimar Republic. While still only in his thirties he won a
reputation as a leading scholar in the field of modern history. With the
coming of the Third Reich he emigrated to the United States, where he
became professor at Yale University. He dealt in his writings with the Re-
naissance and Reformation, with diplomatic history and the philosophy of
history, as well as with Germany. His treatment of Bismarck is not unap-
preciative, but it avoids the uncritical adulation of so many of the Iron
Chancellor's biographers. Here he examines the ideas and ideals which
shaped the mind of the statesman.*

In a famous letter to Leopold von Gerlach Bismarck expressed his
belief that "nobody ever loses the stamp which the age of youthful
impressions has imposed on him," and he distanced himself from
the older man who had formed his ideals during the war of liberation from Napoleon. Friedrich Meinecke already has called attention
to the relatively cool attitude which Bismarck always displayed with
regard to the period of Prussian reform and liberation. To be sure,
the struggle against foreign domination seemed to him a worthy
cause, but he denied that the simultaneous attempt of the Prussian
reformers to establish an ideal German state had made an essential
contribution to eventual liberation. The philosophical idealism of
the age of Kant, Fichte, and Schleiermacher, in which a Stein, Humboldt, Scharnhorst, Gneisenau, and Boyen had found the expression
of their own ideal longings, was alien to Bismarck.

Bismarck grew up when the German philosophy of the classic age

From Hajo Holborn, "Bismarck's Realpolitik," *Journal of the History of Ideas* 21
(1960): 84–91. Reprinted by permission.

ceased to satisfy the hearts of the young. In the years after 1815, the German philosophy had grown more scholastic, and the deep human experiences which had once led to its creation were largely hidden under a crust of abstract logical thought. The generation which began to take the stage after 1835, the year in which David Friedrich Strauss published his *Life of Jesus,* criticized idealism for its failure to understand the new reality and to give a positive direction to life. Strauss, and those after him, Ludwig Feuerbach, Bruno Bauer, and Karl Marx, all manifested the gathering trend toward realism, which with these Young Hegelians, however, assumed at first an even more intensely rationalistic tinge than with the old Hegel.

It was this rationalism that Bismarck resented. As a youth he had received religious instruction from Schleiermacher, the warm-hearted philosopher and patriotic preacher whose vindication of religion and emphasis on sentiment and feeling had meant to an earlier generation the release from the exclusive rule of reason. Bismarck discovered in Schleiermacher's teachings only an intellectualistic pantheism, which he proceeded to combine with a skepticism that denied the possibility of any human knowledge of God's plan of the world and of the place of the individual in it. This agnosticism, which according to Bismarck derived chiefly from Spinoza and the Stoics, always welled up as one important element in Bismarck's thinking, and particularly in his late years.

Bismarck's search for the concrete beauty of life never fully relieved the boredom and melancholy that his skepticism produced. He was always close to nature. His wide readings in German classic literature and most of all in Shakespeare, as well as the music of Beethoven, gave his imaginative mind models of heroic men and great tragic situations. Shakespeare had been declared the poetic genius by Herder and the young Goethe. Bismarck fully accepted the modern German outlook that originated with the literary revolution of *Sturm und Drang.* He desired passion and sentiment and, therefore, found much of the work of the romantic writers to his liking. Yet it was not the romanticism which looked for an escape from the realities into a realm of artificial beauty or of religion that attracted him, but those romantic efforts that led to a clearer grasp of reality. Through its devotion to the unique value of individuality, romanticism, indeed, prepared the ground for a more realistic study of the world, as the growth of modern historical studies in Germany showed. With sharp and piercing eyes the young Bismarck looked around in his own personal world and early revealed an extraordinary gift for literary narration and characterization.

In the school of romanticism the cult of personality flourished to excess, and in this respect also Bismarck was a true child of his age. For some time Byron was dearer to him than Shakespeare. The young Bismarck gave free reign to his pugnaciousness in dozens of duels, and he plunged headlong into stormy love affairs. Eventually he refused to enter, as a Prussian of his class was expected to do, the government services or make the army his career. "I do not like superiors," he exclaimed, and another time, "I want to make music as I like it or not at all." Thus he withdrew to the family estates, which he managed very effectively. But only part of his energies were engaged. There was time left to resume the search for the meaning of life, and even more to parade his self-confidence before the neighbors by audacious acts of sportsmanship or by extravagant pranks. The unbridled cult of individuality was threatening to corrode any serious purpose of his existence. It was his conversion to a positive theistic Christian view and his marriage, in 1847, that ended this period of life of the "mad Junker," as he had been called.

Bismarck's religious conversion has been much studied. Practically no one has questioned the sincerity of his religious feelings, though many have pointed out that Bismarck's adoption of a theistic faith was closely related to his wish to be accepted by his devout future bride and her Pietistic family. The sudden death of a close friend, Marie von Blanckenburg, and the love for her friend Johanna von Puttkamer naturally gave his questions about life a new urgency, and the religion of his friends made a serious impression on him. Still, there was a strong voluntaristic side to Bismarck's decision. By embracing a personal God he set an end to his drifting in doubts. At the same time his marriage gave him a firm anchorage in Prussian society, in which he had his natural roots, but from which so far he had longed to flee into a world of free and heroic action. Together with his pantheism he dismissed what he occasionally called his republicanism. In the same breath he won a wife and a religious and political faith. He had chosen his fundamental position when a little later the revolution drew him into the political arena, first as a parliamentarian, subsequently as a diplomat, and finally as a minister of state.

Yet before appraising his statecraft we must stress that Bismarck did not become a Pietist in 1847. He placed his trust in a personal God, whom he accepted as the creator and king of the universe, but he obviously cared little for Christian dogmas. He prayed to God, whose ways he considered unfathomable and whom he did not think to move by his prayer. But he said—probably unaware that the words could be found in Schleiermacher's *Glaubenslehre*—that the usefulness of prayer lay in submission to a strong power. His new belief in a personal God was actually still compatible with much of Bismarck's original skepticism. Though less general, it was almost as subjective as his earlier notions. As a matter of fact, in his later years he seems to have moved even closer to his early ideas.

It was probably impossible in nineteenth century German Protestantism to find any conception of the Christian Church as a divinely ordained community which possessed a moral authority independent of the state. The Protestant churches were essentially state-controlled institutes for preaching. The Pietists were critics of this state-system and often opposed to ministers. But all they could do was to form small conventicles such as those in which Bismarck had come in contact with Pietistic orthodoxy. Bismarck never cultivated any group worship after his conversion and favored the state-church, though he himself, as he put it, did not wish to be "edified by mouth of ministers." Yet since he suspected ministers of being desirous of power, he preferred having them under the supervision of the state. Another observation can be made. The new faith helped to give Bismarck's whole thinking a firm orientation. It also made him act not only with greater determination but also with a heightened sense of moral responsibility. Yet it did not change his relations with his fellow-men. He remained the cavalier, normally polite to his equals, well-mannered and benevolent even to members of the lesser classes, but on the other hand reckless in forcing people to serve him or humiliating them if they refused, or were suspected of refusing, cooperation. The man who lay awake whole nights "hating," who could perhaps forget but not forgive—all this according to his own testimony—had not through his conversion become a new man.

Friedrich Meinecke has suggested that the decline of German idealism in the 1830s might be responsible for Bismarck's turning away from idealism to orthodoxy and thereby from liberalism to conservatism. He thought that if Bismarck had found a philosophy which would have answered the burning questions of his personal growth, he might have become a more liberal statesman like Cavour. Although I agree with Meinecke that the formation of Bismarck's personal convictions cannot be explained outside of his age, the question raised by Meinecke defies a solution because it is impossible to visualize different historical circumstances while assuming that the person involved would remain the same. Bismarck actually absorbed certain influences of German idealism, and the subjective and voluntaristic religion which he adopted was clearly "post-idealistic," but the liberal and humanitarian elements of the classic German philosophy found no response in him.

In 1838 the young Gladstone wrote his first book in which he pleaded for the closest relation between church and state. Without a sanctifying principle, he argued, the state would become a mere machine with no other function than that of registering and executing opinions of the popular will like the hands of a clock. Gladstone was then still an ardent Tory, and his theses were warmly applauded by Frederick William IV of Prussia and his conservative friends. It is well known how greatly Gladstone's political views changed in his later years, when he became a liberal out of Christian convictions. But as little as he gave up his Christian belief did he deviate from his early demand that creative politics called for "sanctifying principles." Bismarck saw in Gladstone more than in any other statesman on the contemporary European scene his ideological opposite. He was wrong, however, in asserting that Gladstone—or, as he labelled him with one of his strongest vituperative expressions, *"Professor"* Gladstone—was ruining England, nor could he know that a Gladstonean Professor Wilson was destined to become the foremost destroyer of the German monarchy.

What made Bismarck a fiery enemy of Gladstone was both the liberalism and insistence of Gladstone on a Christian program in politics. Bismarck soon parted company with his early conservative associates, the members of the so-called Christian-Germanic circle, with regard to the application of Christian principles to practical politics. In Bismarck's view, the world and its orders were created by God and the course of history directed by him. The existing political institutions, consequently, were not made by men nor could they be altered by ideal constructions of human reason, as the liberals proposed. But the concrete plan of God was unknown to man, except that it was clear that in all history the decisions had been reached by power used for selfish interests, and that this *raison d'état* could be studied and acted upon. This nature of the political life of the world was to him divinely instituted and, therefore, essentially immutable, although life was a continuous conflict and struggle. To hope that men could change the nature of politics would be sinfully arrogant and would mean to meddle in divine government. The statesman might gain, however, at rare moments a fleeting adumbration of divine action on a higher plane.

These ideas excluded the possibility of Christianizing the state and the international life. There was no ideal state, let alone an ideal international order, but only the concrete order of history which demanded from everybody obedience to the positive law. This Bismarckian attitude has been called Lutheran by historical students of Bismarck, and it is quite true that his political conceptions showed the earmarks of the political thinking that had developed in German Lutheranism. But it would be erroneous to assume that Bismarck's and Luther's opinions were identical. The world of states was for Luther not the arena for the realization of the kingdom of God. Luther admitted that statecraft required special political knowledge though to him this was not identical with the *raison d'état*. And while Luther did not believe that the state as such was a Christian institution, he considered it the duty of every individual Christian to assert within the public life a special moral attitude derived from his Christian faith. In this respect Bismarck's early conservative companions, particularly Friedrich Julius Stahl, were closer to Luther than Bismarck.

But Bismarck did not deny that at least the statesman himself, if he was a Christian, was bound by certain specific principles. The exercise of power was not to aim at personal ends but was a calling to preserve the natural order of things and to serve the state. No doubt, these were important moral restraints which reflected genuine ideas of Luther, though in somewhat weaker fashion. Luther justified war only in self-defense and recommended that Christian princes should rather suffer some occasional injustice and forget about their own "reputation" than go to a war that would bring calamitous suffering to their people. Bismarck repeatedly condemned preventive wars and never accepted war lightheartedly, but he did accept it as a means for accomplishing his political aims. Also, he ruled out wars for prestige, but not for the honor of the state.

The outlook on life and history with which Bismarck entered politics endowed the prevailing political conditions of Prussia with an aura of sanctity. Not only the monarchy but also the traditional class society of Prussia, with the Junker estate as the dominant social group, was in his eyes the God-willed order of things, and its maintenance by all means of political cunning the unquestionable duty of the statesman. Liberalism, which for him comprised every movement derived from the ideas of the American and French revolutions, was the sworn enemy of a healthy political life, since it attempted to replace historically developed forms of life by an arbitrary system of man-made institutions. In Bismarck's thought any kind of liberalism was bound to lead to government by parties, and this weakening of the authority of the state would bring forth the chaos of a social republic, from which a people could be freed only by a regime of fire and sword. On the other hand, a regime of naked force was disliked by Bismarck, although many governmental measures which he recommended or adopted were of highly doubtful legality. He was not even a champion of an unrestricted absolute monarchy. He objected to the suppression of the independent rights of the nobility by rulers. Moreover, absolutism fed that "boa constrictor," bureaucracy, which was tyrannical but at the same time a breeding ground of liberal notions.

These Bismarckian conceptions might have made this Junker a radical reactionary after the breakdown of the German revolution, radical to the extent of demanding the suppression of those moderate German-national and liberal trends that had existed in Prussia before 1848, and even more of the concessions made during the revolution, of which the Prussian constitution of 1850 was the most important grant. But in spite of his brazenly contemptuous attitude towards democracy and liberalism during the revolution, Bismarck was not found among the extreme die-hards in the 1850s. A parliament, in particular, seemed to offer many potential advantages. Through it the conservatives could assert their views—if need be even against crown and bureaucracy—and Bismarck never forgot that the king had faltered in the early months of the revolution. But the chief value of a parliament was the chance it provided for entering on a contest with the liberal forces. Bismarck realized that these forces could not be conquered by mere repression and that the ideological errors and the political futility of modern democracy would have to be shown up by word and deed.

While Bismarck, therefore, accepted a parliament, he remained a deadly foe of parliamentary government. The monarchical government was always to retain a basis of power of its own and for this reason never surrender its exclusive control of the army and foreign affairs. During the revolution of 1848–1849 Bismarck had seen that the Austrian and Prussian monarchies recovered their strength because their armies remained loyal to the dynastic cause. He had also observed the weaknesses in German liberalism, how the fear of social revolution had impaired its aggressive spirit, how the political moderates and radicals had divided, and how the ideas about the forms of the desired national union, *grossdeutsch* vs. *kleindeutsch,* had produced further splits in German liberalism. He had also noticed that the social and economic program of the liberals failed to keep its early large following united, and that individual groups could be bought rather cheaply by the old governments. It had not escaped his attention that the majority of the German people, especially the peasant and working classes, were still politically quiescent and that it might be feasible to mobilize them for the support of monarchical government, as Louis Bonaparte had done.

Arnold Oskar Meyer

THE ROAD TO DAMASCUS

Among the writers on Bismarck admirers have far outnumbered critics. Much of the veneration of the Iron Chancellor is idolatry pure and simple, yet sometimes it leads to important research. For a conservative German historian like Arnold Oskar Meyer the great man could do no wrong. He was good, wise, reasonable, patriotic, idealistic, dedicated, and always right. Until his death in 1944 the disciple never tired of singing the praises of his master. But he also wrote the best account of Bismarck's years in Frankfurt as the representative of Prussia at the Diet of the German Confederation. It was during this important period of his life that the Junker of Schönhausen became a convert to the cause of German unification under the Hohenzollerns.

"It was a time when nothing happened." That was how Bismarck during the war of 1870–1871 characterized the period of the German Confederation to which he himself had put an end. He was thinking particularly of the years before 1848, of the absence of great political deeds and events which could exalt the German people above the petty world of commonplace affairs, which could endow their existence with a higher meaning. The only major political achievement of that time, the establishment of the economic unity of Germany through the Zollverein, was won silently and slowly, without the participation of the public at large, and only gradually was its significance recognized. As long as the yearning for the national unification of Germany remained unsatisfied, popular political attitudes were by and large negative. Criticism of the loose structure of the German Confederation, of the backward constitutionalism of north Germany, of the lack of political justice and freedom of expression was much stronger than any positive sense of accomplishment, stronger than the joyful realization that in spite of everything conditions were visibly improving, stronger than pride in the flourishing intellectual life of the universities and the leading position of German scholarship in the world. Only after the artificial system of the German Confederation, that great disappointment of 1815, seemed

From Arnold Oskar Meyer, *Bismarcks Kampf mit Österreich am Bundestag zu Frankfurt* (1851 *bis* 1859) (Berlin and Leipzig, 1927), pp. 12–16, 503–506. Reprinted by permission of K. F. Koehler Verlag. Translated by Theodore S. Hamerow and William W. Beyer.

to vanish forever during the stormy spring of 1848, making way for the creation of a German Empire, only then did men finally begin to believe that they could feel the breath of a new, greater, and better time. The hope proved deceptive. Seldom or never in the history of a great nation was a reaction met with greater aversion and hopelessness than that which began with the restoration of the Diet of the German Confederation in Frankfurt after the failure of the work of unification. The struggle had been all in vain. The time when nothing happened was to come back. The bitter hatred or dull indifference of a crushed generation greeted the return of the old days, which weighed like a shroud on the bier of the stillborn German Empire in the middle of the nineteenth century.

It was precisely this time which led the creator of the new Germany to his proper sphere of action. Until 1850 Otto von Bismarck had been able to act politically only in parliament and through the press. Even then he belonged in the first rank, being the most richly endowed in intelligence, courage, and political insight of his party. Yet he was still far from the center of power, he was still without influence over the course of policy. Only his entry into the diplomatic service brought him the first taste of that influence. Bismarck's career as a diplomat, however, began exactly at the place where the great majority of Germans saw the grave of their national aspirations, in the Palace of the Confederation in Frankfurt am Main. For nearly eight years, from May (in charge only from August) 1851 until February 1859 Bismarck represented the Prussian government in the Diet of the German Confederation. They were eight years of almost uninterrupted struggle with the presiding power of the Confederation, with Prussia's ancient rival, the Austrian imperial state; they were eight years of constant training and growing maturity arising out of that struggle. He assumed his post "in a state of political innocence," as he described it ten years later. When he had to leave it again against his will at the very moment which he thought would finally bring him the prize of victory, the overthrow of Austria as leader of the German Confederation, he had acquired not only the outward expertness which he had at first lacked, not only the complete mastery of diplomatic forms, not only a knowledge of men and affairs which led his government to recognize him as a great authority on European as well as German questions. More important,

through the flexibility, the breadth, and the discernment of his outlook he had outgrown all his party friends. In his mind lay hidden
plans so bold and grand that none of Prussia's professional diplo-
mats had dared think them.

Bismarck the man as well as the statesman later fondly recalled
his years at Frankfurt. "How could I help being well-disposed toward
a city where I spent so many happy hours and where I met so many
charming people." But he permitted the publication of his political
reports from Frankfurt while he was still in office as a leading statesman, an unusual step for him. After his dismissal an invaluable supplement appeared, Bismarck's correspondence with Adjutant General
Leopold von Gerlach, which with his reports constitutes an incom-
parable source for the development of his political genius. It was thus
already possible during Bismarck's lifetime to study his years of
apprenticeship as depicted in his own accounts. But however clear
and profound the images which this mirror reflects, they must still
be supplemented. Only if we also know how the portrait of the great
fighter looked to the eye of the stranger, above all to the eye of the
political opponent, can we approach historical accuracy as closely
as scholarly research and imagination make possible. The main significance of Bismarck's activity in Frankfurt lay in the struggle with
Austria. The reports of his Austrian colleagues therefore constitute
the most important supplement to his own reports. Only through the
testimony of his adversaries, for whom he admittedly did not make
life easy, can we fully understand how young Bismarck, the maturing
statesman, fought. We see his carefully restrained and yet at times
still undisciplined strength engaged in the creative deed; we experience with him that wonderful time of life which combines the last
charm of youth with the full strength of early manhood.

He went to Frankfurt as the representative of a humbled state.
Prussia had failed in everything, in everything except the taming of
the revolution. She had failed in her German policy, she had failed
in Schleswig-Holstein, she had failed in the attempt to meet the
expectations of her own as well as of the German people by the
introduction of a constitutional form of government. On the other
hand, Austria, with whose representative Bismarck was now to sit
at the same table, had emerged victorious from even greater disas-
ters. She was the victor over the revolution in her own country; victor

over uprisings in Italy and Hungary, although in the latter case with Russian assistance; victor finally over Prussia's German policy. Bismarck's mission was to defend the rights and the dignity of the deeply humiliated Prussian state against this Austria. There was no mission in the entire Prussian diplomatic service more difficult and more responsible.

When asked, Bismarck accepted it without hesitation or doubt. "I cannot withdraw without becoming a deserter." He went to Frankfurt as the soldier of God. "Wherever He sends me, that is where I must go. And I believe that He is sending me and shaping my life as He sees fit." The career for which the youth had longed was now opened to the grown man, although he had done nothing to win the appointment, he had not even uttered a word to express his wishes. Yet besides the joyous creative impulse and sense of power with which he entered upon the great stage there was also something almost sad, the realization that he was leaving the life of the countryside. "I feel as if we were emigrating to America and parting from all our dear, familiar ways. For who knows when the wheel which has now seized us will release us again, and we will once more spend a quiet summer in the country." When the wheel finally did release him against his will, the old man left behind him a world which his deeds had transformed. . . .

There is a portrait of the man done in 1855, when he was at the height of his power in the Diet, when Austria was isolated and Prussia led the other states of Germany. The portrait was painted by an artist who knew Bismarck and his family. Here is no longer the youthful champion with blond, luxuriant beard, whose appearance and conduct aroused the criticism of elders, looking schoolboyish by diplomatic standards. This is a man of the world, elegant, well-bred, confident, a master of others as of himself. The fire of his youth is still there, the daring courage and the self-assurance. There is lightning in the blue eyes. They gaze at the world full of the joy of life, sparkling with spirit and wit, and with a sharpness of perception which seems to pierce all pretense. There is no prouder bearing than that portrayed in the picture, but pride is the heart and soul of the man. He has at his command the enormous intellectual powers mirrored in these features. This man knows that he is superior to all others; he has never met anyone who could surpass him. And he is second to none in the strength of his will. Rarely has nature shaped a jaw expressing such energy.

It is the portrait of a fighter who knows no fear, powerful and tough, clever and cunning. The once radiant blond hair is thinning, it looks darker on that mighty north German skull of the man of forty. But the rosy, almost delicate complexion retains the color of youthfulness and health. Life in all its fullness is still before him. In a photograph taken about the time of his departure from Frankfurt . . . the clear gaze is directed upward, as if toward some high goal in the distance. The struggles which lie behind him, struggles such as the Diet of the Confederation had never seen before and would never see again, were only the first great test of his strength.

He, who as an inexperienced beginner had been assigned to the most difficult post, passed the test as perhaps no diplomat had ever done. When in May 1851 the newspapers reported that Deputy von Bismarck-Schönhausen was being sent to the Diet of the Confederation in Frankfurt, the satirical journal *Kladderadatsch* made jokes about the appointment. What the public knew about him in those days was by and large only that there was no speaker on any platform more cutting than he, and that in all of Prussia no one was a more valiant defender of the rights of the crown. Those who knew him better realized something else. Marie de la Motte-Fouqué, daughter of the romanticist and niece of Rochow, Bismarck's predecessor at Frankfurt, wrote in her diary:

> *What Theodor (von Rochow) will be able to make out of his pupil Bismarck time alone can tell. All those who know him well say that he will certainly not be lacking in knowledge, ability, savoir-faire, cunning, and astuteness in handling people.*

Bismarck's colleagues in Frankfurt were to be of two minds on this last point. But any blunders in dealing with them which he may have committed through excessive gruffness harmed only him, not his state.

What he did for Prussia in Frankfurt was much; what he wanted to do was very much more. He kept Prussia from sinking into dependence on Austria, from losing her power for decision. Thereby he nullified the effects of the defeat at Olmütz, of the treaty which he himself had once defended in a brilliant speech in the legislature. But he wanted more. He wanted to lead his state back to the policy of the great Frederick, to the policy ~~of conquest, the conquest of~~ Germany. "Their skin is too tight for them," Prokesch-Osten used to say about the Prussians, and the phrase was apt. Just as once Crown Prince Frederick at Küstrin, waiting for his hour to strike, studied the map in order to dooido where to make his conquests, so for many years Bismarck often sat in front of his maps of Germany, silent, shrouded in clouds of smoke, before his destiny called him. An embrasure with an old sewing table in the living room of the manor house at Schönhausen was his favorite spot. "There sits Hercules holding a distaff," his wife's mother once commented while passing through the room. That was in the fall of 1847. He could not free himself from the thought that Prussia must grow. In his speech on Olmütz he had regretfully remarked: "We are not interested in conquests." But he hinted that he would be prepared for war if his king said: "I like this land and I want to possess it." In Frankfurt he spoke rather carelessly during the Crimean War about Prussia's need to expand not in Poland, but in Germany, Saxony, and Hanover. And his dreams of conquest rose to dizzy heights during Austria's troubles in the spring of 1859.

In Frankfurt Bismarck had come to know federalism in its most calamitous form. He therefore wanted to cauterize the wound with a red-hot iron. And there were many voices in 1866 which regretted that this cauterization was not even more drastic than Bismarck had made it. We cannot compare his achievement in its final form with what was only a thought at the time of his departure from Frankfurt. For there are only a few flashes of light illuminating that thought, like lightning on a stormy night. What they reveal and what they suggest shows the boldness of a Frederick the Great, but not yet the maturity of Bismarckian wisdom which is displayed only in the completed work. The German Hercules still stood only at the beginning of his accomplishments; the greatest and most difficult of them still lay before him.

A. J. P. Taylor
A FREUDIAN APPROACH

Interest in the Iron Chancellor is not confined to German historians. The well-known English scholar A. J. P. Taylor has written a highly critical biography, portraying his protagonist as a gifted neurotic driven by a need to satisfy his colossal ego. Here is a Bismarck who cannot be interpreted simply as a Prussian Junker, or a Pietistic Lutheran, or even a bold diplomat crossing swords with mighty Austria. His brilliant but unstable personality must be described in the language of psychoanalysis. Taylor writes with such urbanity and assurance that like St. Paul he almost persuades us.

His father Ferdinand was a typical Junker, sprung from a family as old as the Hohenzollerns—"a Swabian family no better than mine" Bismarck once remarked. Schönhausen itself symbolized their humiliation; for they had received it as compensation for their original family estate, which a Hohenzollern elector had coveted and seized. The Bismarcks had done nothing to gain distinction during their long feudal obscurity. Ferdinand did not even exert himself to fight for his king. He left the Prussian army at 23; and missed both the disastrous Jena campaign in 1806 and the War of Liberation against Napoleon in 1813. The efficient management of his rambling estates was beyond him, and he drifted helplessly into economic difficulties. It needed a vivid imagination for the son to turn this easy-going, slow-witted man, with his enormous frame, into a hero, representing all that was best in Prussian tradition.

Wilhelmine, the mother, was a different character. Her family, the Menkens, were bureaucrats without a title, not aristocrat landowners. Some of them had been university professors. Her father was a servant of the Prussian state, prized by Frederick the Great and later in virtual control of all home affairs. His reforms and quick critical spirit brought down on him the accusation of "Jacobinism." Wilhelmine was a town-child, at home only in the drawing rooms of Berlin. She had a sharp, restless intellect, which roamed without system from Swedenborg to Mesmer. At one moment she would be discussing the latest works of political liberalism; at the next dabbling in spiritualist experiments. Married to Ferdinand von Bismarck at sixteen, she developed interest neither for her heavy husband nor in country life. All her hopes were centered on her children. They were to achieve the intellectual life that had been denied to her. Her only ambition, she said, was to have "a grown-up son who would penetrate far further into the world of ideas than I, as a woman, have been able to do."

She gave her children encouragement without love. She drove them on; she never showed them affection. Otto, the younger son, inherited her brains. He was not grateful for the legacy. He wanted love from her, not ideas; and he was resentful that she did not share his admiration for his father. It is a psychological commonplace for a son to feel affection for his mother and to wish his father out of the way. The results are more interesting and more profound when a son, who takes after his mother, dislikes her character and standards of value. He will seek to turn himself into the father with whom he has little in common, and he may well end up neurotic or a genius. Bismarck was both. He was the clever, sophisticated son of a clever, sophisticated mother, masquerading all his life as his heavy, earthy father.

Even his appearance showed it. He was a big man, made bigger by his persistence in eating and drinking too much. He walked stiffly, with the upright carriage of a hereditary officer. Yet he had a small, fine head; the delicate hands of an artist; and when he spoke, his voice, which one would have expected to be deep and powerful, was thin and reedy—almost a falsetto—the voice of an academic, not of a man of action. Nor did he always present the same face to the world. He lives in history clean-shaven, except for a heavy mustache. Actually he wore a full beard for long periods of his life; and this at a time when beards were symbols on the continent of Europe of the romantic movement, if not of radicalism. In the use of a razor, as in other things, Bismarck sometimes followed Metternich, sometimes Marx. Despite his Junker mien, he had the sensitivity of a woman, incredibly quick in responding to the moods of another, or even in anticipating them. His conversational charm could bewitch tsars, queens and revolutionary leaders. Yet his great strokes of policy came after long solitary brooding, not after discussion with others. Indeed he never exchanged ideas in the usual sense of the term. He gave orders or, more rarely, carried them out; he did not cooperate. In a life of conflict, he fought himself most of all. He said once: "Faust complains of having two souls in his breast. I have a whole squabbling crowd. It goes on as in a republic." When someone asked him if he were really the Iron Chancellor, he replied: "Far from it. I am all nerves, so much so that self-control has always been the greatest task of my life and still is." He willed himself into a line of policy or action. His friend Keyserling noted of his conversion to religion: "Doubt was not fought and conquered; it was silenced by heroic will."

He felt himself always out of place, solitary and a stranger to his surroundings. "I have the unfortunate nature that everywhere I could be seems desirable to me, and dreary and boring as soon as I am there." He loathed the intellectual circles of Berlin to which his mother introduced him, and in 1848 said to a liberal politician: "I am a Junker and mean to have the advantages of that position." But the years he spent as a Junker, managing his estates, were the most miserable of his life; and when, as chancellor, he retired to his beloved countryside, he was happy only so long as the state papers continued to pour in on him. He spent the twenty-eight years of supreme power announcing his wish to relinquish it; yet no man has left office with such ill grace or fought so unscrupulously to recover it. He despised writers and literary men; yet only Luther and Goethe rank with him as masters of German prose. He found happiness only in his family; loved his wife, and gave to his children the affection that he had been denied by his mother. He said in old age that his greatest good fortune was "that God did not take any of my children from me." Yet he ruined the happiness of his adored elder son for the sake of a private feud, and thought nothing of spending a long holiday away from his wife in the company of a pretty girl; indeed he was so self-centered that he boasted to his wife of the girl's charm and good looks. He claimed to serve sometimes the king of Prussia, sometimes Germany, sometimes God. All three were cloaks for his own will; and he turned against them ruthlessly when they did not serve his purpose. He could have said with Oliver Cromwell, whom he much resembled: "He goeth furthest who knows not whither he is going." The young Junker had no vision that he would unify Germany on the basis of universal suffrage; and the maker of three wars did not expect to end as the great buttress of European peace.

Bismarck was not brought up as a Junker, despite his constant assertions of this character in later life. The family moved soon after he was born to the smaller estate of Kniephof in Pomerania. Here there was a smaller house with no architectural pretensions and hard practical farming. The Junkers, unlike the English gentry, did not live on rents. They worked the land themselves, and their peasants were, in reality, agricultural laborers, many of whom did not cultivate any land of their own. Bismarck experienced this idyllic existence only till he was seven. Then his mother set up house in Berlin, no doubt much to her own satisfaction, but ostensibly to send her sons to school in the capital. This exile from the country gave Bismarck a lasting grievance against his mother. The education which she chose for him was another. A Junker's son usually went into a cadet corps and, later, joined a cavalry regiment, even if he was not destined for a permanent military career. Wilhelmine, however, insisted that her children should have an intellectual education suited to the grandsons of the great Menken; and Bismarck went to the best Berlin grammar school of the day where he mixed with the sons of middle-class families. His mother revived her connections with the court; and Bismarck led a privileged existence, mixing on intimate terms with the younger Hohenzollerns. This counted in his later career. Despite his sturdy affectation of independence, he was always inside the royal circle and was treated as one of the family.

The spirit of the Enlightenment still dominated Prussian education; and Bismarck left school "as a Pantheist and if not as a republican, with the belief that a republic was the most reasonable form of state." His mother once more imposed her intellectual standards by sending him out of Prussia to the University of Göttingen in Hanover, the greatest liberal center of the day. Bismarck at first took a radical line. He defied university discipline both in behavior and ideas. What was more, he joined the *Burschenschaften*—students' unions which tried to keep alive the revolutionary spirit of the War of Liberation. He soon turned the other way. It was one thing to pose as a young radical in the court circles of Berlin; quite another to accept these ill-bred students from the middle class as his equals. Personal relations changed Bismarck's political outlook, as was often to happen in his later life. He suddenly discovered pride of blood and joined an aristocratic students-corps. He still led a disorderly existence. He drank a great deal; had some passionate *affaires;* and, like the young Disraeli, wore fantastic and colorful clothes. He was always ready for a duel, though the only time he was injured he characteristically alleged that it was a foul blow—an allegation which he maintained unforgivingly even thirty years later. After three terms, debts drove him back to Berlin, where he could live at home; and here he put in a second academic year. In May 1835, when he was just twenty, he scraped through the examination which qualified him for entry into the Prussian civil service.

Though Bismarck was never a great scholar, his years at the university left their mark. He read widely, despite his boasts of idleness, though he read more history than the law that he was supposed to be studying. He liked Schiller, admired Goethe, and ranked Shakespeare and Byron above either of them—tastes characteristic of the romantic movement. Scott was his greatest favorite of all, romance and history blended in the right proportions. Bismarck's classical learning was scanty; his scientific knowledge almost nonexistent. All the historical references in his speeches are to the three hundred years since the Reformation; his occasional echoes of Darwinism only what he could pick up from a newspaper. Philosophy never interested him; and he was one of the few Germans to escape the influence of Hegel. People were always more important to Bismarck than books. . . .

In 1844 he returned to the Prussian civil service, only to leave it again after a fortnight. His simple explanation was: "I have never been able to put up with superiors." By now he was 30, bitter, cynical and neurotic, his gifts running to nothing. New life came unexpectedly with religion, a wife, and a revolution. Bismarck learnt religion from the only neighbors for whom he cared—devout Lutherans who developed a quietist religion in a Quaker spirit. He was impressed by their content and peaceful confidence. Hoping to discover their secret, he spent much time in their company; and he found there a wife, Johanna von Puttkamer. His open avowal of religious belief was, no doubt, made partly to win her hand. After baring his soul to his prospective father-in-law, he wrote lightheartedly to his sceptical brother:

I think I am entitled to count myself among the adherents of the Christian religion. Though in many doctrines, perhaps in those which they regard as essential, I am far removed from their standpoint, yet a sort of treaty . . . has been silently established between us. Besides, I like piety in women and have a horror of feminine cleverness.

This letter, too, was a piece of diplomacy, with its repudiation of their mother in the last sentence. Yet there can be no doubt that, whatever reserves he might have for his brother, Bismarck's faith became strong and sincere.

His religion was far removed from Christianity, or rather from the humanitarian Christianity of the twentieth century. There was in it little love, except for his own family. He believed in the God of the Old Testament and of the English puritans, the God of battles. Luther or Oliver Cromwell would have understood Bismarck's religion, though it is less easily grasped by those for whom religion is simply a high-flown form of liberalism. Bismarck certainly used war as an instrument of policy and exercised secular power to the full. Anglo-Saxon sentimentalists are therefore inclined to suggest that his religion was sham. Yet the overwhelming majority of Christians have agreed with Bismarck in both theory and practice for nearly two thousand years. Lutheranism especially never claimed to lay down moral principles for public policy. It taught that service to the state and to the appointed ruler was a high religious duty. Bismarck felt this himself: "I believe that I am obeying God when I serve the king." His religion gave to his unstable personality a settled purpose and a sense of power. He said just after Sedan: "You would not have had such a chancellor if I had not the wonderful basis of religion." He believed that he was doing God's work in making Prussia strong and in unifying Germany. The belief itself brought power. God was on his side; therefore he could ignore the opposition of men. Like others who have had this belief, he easily persuaded himself that whatever suited him at the moment was God's purpose and, indeed, that he understood this purpose a great deal better than did God Himself.

Marriage brought to Bismarck lasting and secure happiness. Unlike most men, Bismarck did not marry his mother, but her opposite— a simple, devoted woman, endlessly patient and ready to put up with anything. Under his rough exterior, he was deeply emotional, a man of the romantic movement. He had grown up just when the Byronic legend dominated the Continent. He was the contemporary of Heine and Wagner. Like Gladstone, he was much given to tears at any public or private crisis; no doubt he too would have wept over *East Lynne.* He broke down sobbing after his first public speech and again after the battle of Sadowa. He wept when he became prime minister and even more when he left office. William I and he often sobbed together, though Bismarck always got his way. Music affected him deeply, the more because he could neither play nor read it. And by music he meant a soft glow of feeling when the sonatas of Beethoven were played with more expression than accuracy. He agreed with his wife's verdict on Anton Rubinstein, the greatest pianist of the age: "The playing was masterly both in control and attack and in every-thing you like, and yet 'the heart, the heart remains homeless.' " Johanna gave him a home for his heart, and it was very homely indeed. Though he played high drama on the public stage, his private setting resembled a Victorian boarding-house. Even in that tasteless age contemporaries commented on the banality of Bismarck's sur-roundings.

II TAMER OF PARLIAMENT

Heinrich von Sybel
THE GREAT COMPROMISE

*Among the Prussian liberals who first opposed Bismarck and then supported
him was the prominent historian Heinrich von Sybel. He was rewarded for
his loyal service to the united Germany by being asked to write the semi-
official history of its establishment. The result was the seven volumes of
The Founding of the German Empire by William I. Despite its title, the hero
of the work is not the ruler but his minister. One wit even suggested that
there was a misprint in the name of the book, that it should be "notwith-
standing" instead of "by." Bismarck is portrayed as the soul of moderation
and compromise. A critic complained that Sybel had transformed the tiger
into a pussycat. In the following selection he describes the political consequences of the Prussian victory at Sadowa on July 3, 1866.*

The 3d of July had brought the Prussian government, not only the
overwhelming victory over Austria, but also a telling success against
the opposition at home. At the same time that the Prussian battalions
were annihilating the Austrian army, the opposition suffered such
losses in the elections to the Parliament that the government, whose
party in the years of the constitutional struggle had at times melted
away to ten or twelve members, carried through their candidates for
nearly half of the Lower House. With such a combination of political
and military triumphs how many of the great conquerors of ancient
or modern times would have resisted the temptation to break in
pieces the hostile empire without, and to propose to themselves the
overthrow of all constitutional restraints within.

But Bismarck was made of other stuff. He was not striving for
world-dominion nor for boundless power, but for the means to secure
and strengthen his Prussian Fatherland. So much acquisition of
power and of territory as was necessary for this he laid hold of with
iron grasp—so much and no more. The intoxication of victory never
disordered his judgment, nor got the mastery over his fixed principles of moderation. . . .

The opening of the Parliament was fixed for Sunday noon, August
5th, in the celebrated white hall of the royal palace; and it can easily

From Heinrich von Sybel, *The Founding of the German Empire by William I*, 7 vols.
(New York, 1890–1898), V: 390–391, 404–409, 487–491.

be imagined with what intense suspense the appearance of the king
was awaited. Every one said to himself that the old struggle over the
organization of the army had been ended upon the battlefields of
Bohemia: whoever might still have wished to dispute the intrinsic
value of that creation of King William's would have exposed himself
to everlasting ridicule. But who knew what further use the king would
make of this triumph? The men of the *Kreuzzeitung* party threatened,
and those of the Party of Progress feared, that now a budgetless rule
would be proclaimed to be the only proper system, and any further
opposition would be put down by a dictatorship that had become all-
powerful. The whole existence of the constitution seemed to tremble
in the balance.

Accordingly, on the 5th of August, every one that could offer any
claim whatever to the right to enter the palace sought to gain admis-
sion. All the galleries and boxes around the hall were filled to over-
flowing, and the members of the two Houses were present in unusual
numbers. Soon after twelve o'clock the royal procession arrived; and
at the appearance of the king the excited state of public feeling
manifested itself in tremendous cheers.

The king, with the heir apparent on his right and the ministers on
his left, took his place in front of the throne and began with a loud
voice, amidst the breathless stillness of the audience, to read the
speech. The first clause expressed thanks for God's gracious guid-
ance; and accompanying the especial mention of the heroic deeds
and terrible sacrifices of the nation in arms came the admonition that
a harmonious cooperation of the government and the popular representation might bring to maturity the fruits whose seeds had been so
bedewed with blood. The state of the finances, the king continued,
was brilliant; it had been possible, without extraordinarily burdening
the people, to bring the great war to a glorious conclusion. During
the last year or so, indeed, an agreement as to the budget had not
been arrived at. The public outlay during that time had therefore
lacked that legal authorization, which, as was often admitted, the
department of finance could receive only from the law passed every
year and agreed upon between the government and the representatives of the people. Under these circumstances, the government had
felt itself obliged, without such a law, to make such disbursements as
were indispensable to the maintenance of the state; its conduct had

been the result of an unavoidable necessity, such as a government, in the interest of the country, could not and might not seek to evade. It was, however, to be hoped that in view of recent events the indemnity which the government was about to move would be readily voted; and that thus the conflict that had been kept up hitherto would be terminated for all time; all the more surely was this to be expected since it was believed that the political condition of the Fatherland would permit an enlargement of the boundaries of the state and the establishment of a unified confederate army under the leadership of Prussia.

Though the satisfactory contents and the warm tone of the speech had already occasioned more than once an expression of approval among the hearers, at this point the inward, inspiring sense of freedom from anxiety that was felt by the immense majority of the spectators burst forth in loud and renewed applause. So there was to be no *coup d'état*, no overthrowal of the constitution! The prospect was held out of the restoration of internal peace, not by military authority, but by a simple harmonious settlement: the Lower House recognizing on its part its error in judgment, now so clearly proven, with regard to the new organization of the army, and the crown on its side recognizing anew and confirming the right of the House to determine the budget. The heaviest burden was thus removed from the bosoms of thousands of patriotic men. Now let a foreign disturber of the peace dare to cross the frontier!

The king concluded his speech with these words, which he had added on his own account to the original draft:

Gentlemen! You feel, and the whole Fatherland feels with me, the great importance of the moment which has brought me back among you again. May Providence as graciously bless Prussia in the future as it has visibly done in the immediate past. God grant it may be so!

According to custom, the president of the Upper House answered the royal speech with a thrice repeated *vivat* for the king, in which the assembly joined with a veritable storm of enthusiasm. All hearts were touched. And who could have resisted the impression of the power and the benignity that were stamped on the countenance of the aged ruler?

That the Lower House would not reject the hand that was proffered to it was evident at the very opening of its sessions. During the whole continuance of the constitutional struggle, the president had been Grabow, a man by no means of radically democratic tendencies, but passionately excited by the violation of his sense of right. He had frequently from the presidential chair given violent expression to his convictions concerning the unconstitutional course pursued by the government. He now with noble self-abnegation expressed to the House his desire that his re-election should not be considered, so that his name might not be an obstacle in the way of reconciliation.

Thereupon, Von Forckenbeck, the candidate of the parties that had hitherto constituted the opposition, was elected by 170 votes against 136 of the Conservatives and 22 of the Old Liberals. There was therefore now, as before, no ministerial party with a certain majority; but, nevertheless, the election of Forckenbeck proclaimed the victory of moderate tendencies and conciliatory principles even in the circles of modern and advanced liberalism. For in the very beginning of the constitutional struggle Forckenbeck, by bringing up motions for amendment and for conciliation, had stood in marked contrast with the purely negative attitude of Waldeck and his associates. The election of such a man was the first symptom of a new formation of parties with a tendency at once liberal and national.

Violent and bitter as the feeling had been during the conflict, it was no longer possible not to see that the government and the Liberals were pursuing the same object, and that for the normal establishment of the German state the power of the government was quite as needful as the general agitation of public sentiment. Whoever was in earnest on the subject of German unity was bound to declare himself, willingly or unwillingly, an ally of the government in the question which controlled the whole life of Germany; and, consequently, whoever was in earnest about the practical realization of liberal ideas was bound to make up his mind to cooperate actively with the government, in order not to leave the new arrangement of the German state entirely to his political opponents. For four years the constitutional struggle had united the great mass of the Liberals with the Radical Democrats, and had thus cut off the former from any share in the furtherance of the German cause. From the moment when circumstances rendered possible the settlement of that constitutional struggle, this unnatural alliance began to be dissolved. Independent of the Radical groups there arose once more a Liberal party, now brought upon the side of the government by the German question, but at the same time independent in its principles, and soon to grow largely in numbers and in influence. . . .

The government had already, on the 14th of August, sent to the House the draft of an indemnity bill, containing the motion to grant to the ministry of state indemnity for the expenses incurred during the years 1862–1865, a general outline of which was appended; while for the year 1866, since the state of things was no longer adapted to the establishment of a regular budget, the government desired a loan of 154 million thalers. In the budget committee, to whose consideration the matter was referred, it was very soon evident that a large majority favored the acceptance of the bill.

The only determined opposition came from the members of the Party of Progress, who were not able to find in the draft of the bill the necessary security for the reestablishment of constitutional rights. These, therefore, approved the loan for 1866, but wished to decline for the present the proposal about the indemnity and to leave it with the government to make the request again after the budget for 1867 should have been fixed upon.

To this the reply was made that if the present promise of the government to adopt the budget for 1867 were not to be trusted, then the passage and adoption of this latter could not be looked upon as a sure guaranty for the acceptance of a regular budget for 1868. The main thing, it was asserted, was the serious intention of the government to return to the basis of the constitution; and this determination was believed to be sufficiently indicated in the bill. The whole dispute arose, it was said, from a difference of opinion about the new organization of the army, and who could at this late day think of undertaking any essential changes in the same? For, indeed, it was very probable that if it had been possible to foresee the last war and its consequences, the House would not have thought of refusing its approval to the new military constitution. The matter of the organization of the army must be settled anew, it was argued, by a definite law; but such a law would not under the existing state of things have to be passed by the Prussian Lower House but by the North German

Parliament. The report revised by Deputy Twesten in accordance with these sentiments was adopted by the committee by a vote of twenty-five to eight.

In the House the discussion was, as ever, more lively, and the views more sharply opposed to one another. The whole Party of Progress set themselves determinedly against the bill. Waldeck considered that nothing whatever had been offered that justified any expectation of more constitutional conduct on the part of the government. Schultze-Delitzsch declared that the whole war had been carried on not only without the consent, but even against the will, of the Prussian people; and he was naive enough to refer to those melancholy addresses of peace of May and June as a brilliant proof of Prussia's careful prudence compared with the tumult of war which prevailed then at Vienna.

Virchow explained that he and his friends had known a better way leading to German unity than Bismarck's, namely, the way of freedom. But as things now stood, he said, they were willing to sacrifice their wishes to Bismarck, and were willing to support his foreign policy, but must so much the more energetically defend constitutional rights. As if Benedek in June would have allowed himself to be deterred from marching upon Berlin by the fiery enthusiasm of the Party of Progress for freedom! or as if there could have been at this time any worse foe to Bismarck's German policy conceivable than the continuance of the internal quarrel! The professor of Catholic theology, Michelis, supplemented these remarks by the brilliant observation that Tetzel in 1517 was accused unjustly for having sold indulgences for future sins, but that this bill did indeed involve a pardon for all the future sins of the ministry.

The Conservative party, delighted at the favorable sentiments, declared with great ardor that it would vote for the indemnity-bill in accordance with the wishes of the government, although strictly speaking, something entirely different would be more properly in order, namely, a hearty vote of thanks to the government for not having taken account of the foolish behavior of the House. The mediatory position held by Bismarck and Von der Heydt also received eloquent support from the parties of the Center. Lasker and Georg Vincke, at other times seldom to be found on the same side, and also, at the close of the discussion, Twesten, who had made the report, demonstrated with convincing force the importance of the present situation, the consequence of a continued quarrel with the government, and the power of public opinion which demanded unity of action.

The final vote on the report resulted in 230 in favor and 75 against, the latter including the Party of Progress, some few members of the Left Center, and the Catholic fraction. The Upper House followed this example on the 8th of September, after Herr von Kleist-Retzow had given vent to his regrets at the injurious compliance on the part of the government. The vote of the Upper House resulted in the unanimous acceptance of the bill as drawn up by the House of Deputies.

Internal peace was thus secured and the four years' contest over the constitution was ended. With good practical sense, that question which lay at the very bottom of the quarrel, namely, what was to happen if again sometime the budget should not be passed, was left to future decision; and it was considered sufficient to heal the present wound by mutually trusting to the royal word: "It will not happen again."

Since then more than twenty years have passed. Often enough have the representatives of the people refused to pass bills presented by the government; but they have never found any reason to doubt the loyalty of the ministers to the constitution. It has not happened again. And may it not happen again, that the popular representation on its part shall occasion such an urgent condition of things that the welfare of the state shall be the only law in force!

Otto Pflanze
LIBERALISM SURRENDERS

Not all scholars agree that the reconciliation of crown and parliament in Prussia in 1866 represented the triumph of sweet reasonableness over dogmatism and partisanship. Otto Pflanze, professor of history at the University of Minnesota, suggests in his learned and discerning biography of Bismarck that the liberals lost more than they won by approving the bill of indemnity. They may have thought that by their capitulation they would gain the opportunity to participate in the creation of a new civic order in their country. In fact they sacrificed their principles for a mess of pottage, for a spurious parliamentarism and an egocentric nationalism. Their surrender to success helped reinforce the tradition of authority in Germany which led to war and defeat in the twentieth century.

On August 5, 1866 the white hall of the palace . . . was crowded with deputies, the political atmosphere completely changed. Popular support, for which the opposition had angled so long, was now overwhelmingly on the side of the monarchy. The army, whose reorganization they had opposed and whose financial support they had denied, was brilliantly victorious. Its officers were the Junkers against whose power they had striven in vain. Its commander-in-chief was the king whose ministers had violated the constitution and frustrated the parliamentary will. Back of the whole conservative order, furthermore, loomed the sentiment of German nationalism. In seven weeks dynasty, ministers, army, and Junkers had taken a mighty step toward the realization of the liberal dream of half a century. Achievement of the rest was assumed to be but a matter of time. Now the government announced its willingness to come halfway toward the settlement of the constitutional conflict.

The situation was powerfully persuasive. That the liberals were so strongly affected by it, however, was not merely owing to the dramatic events of June and July 1866. Their capitulation had been prepared for more than a century in the development of the German liberal tradition. Its origin lay in the delayed growth of the German

From "The Conquest of Prussia," in Otto Pflanze, *Bismarck and the Development of Germany*, vol. I, *The Period of Unification, 1815–1871* (copyright 1963 by Princeton University Press; Princeton Paperback, 1971), pp. 326–331. Reprinted by permission of Princeton University Press.

middle class, the peculiar coupling of freedom and authority, the dualism of Kantian thought, the Hegelian deification of the state, and the romantic glorification of force. The liberals were the victims of their own limited ends, their lack of genuine popular support, and their lust for national power. What they had desired was not a fundamental change of the existing political structure, but merely the validation of the "mixed constitution." Never had they aimed at full responsibility for the management of public affairs. Theirs had been a purely defensive action, for the *Rechtsstaat* against the encroachments of arbitrary government. As in 1848 they feared the masses, and as in 1848 the masses were not behind them.

As early as 1864 they had displayed a fatal hunger for military success and foreign expansion; now they found this but an appetizer for the main course. Theirs had been the illusion that wars for great objectives could be fought only with their own support. But the unbelievable had happened. The supposed spokesman of reactionary conservatism had not only steered the country into a major war, but had summoned the nation to accomplish its unity under the protective umbrella of Prussian power. Again the Prussian state had stolen the most vital planks of the liberal platform. Bureaucratic liberalism had preempted once more the program of moderate liberalism. To most there now appeared no other place to stand than upon or under the inviting new structure Bismarck was busily building with stolen materials.

For many the conversion was not difficult. Wehrenpfennig concluded, "Bismarck is, except for Stein, the greatest statesman Prussia has ever had; it appears that he is luckier and perhaps even bolder than the latter." Rudolf Ihering, Göttingen professor of law, who earlier had denounced the war as an act of "frightful frivolity," now bowed down before the "genius of a Bismarck," declaring that for such a man of deeds he would give one hundred of impotent honesty. Almost overnight the Bismarck cult was born. Its devotees began to reinterpret their hero's actions during the preceding four years. They excused his infringements of the constitution in view of what was presumed to have been his hidden purpose. Impatiently the liberal press, so bitterly hostile from March to June, now pressed the deputies not to hinder the government in the fulfillment of its "duty" toward the rest of Germany. In view of the "glorious" work

ahead, the issues of the constitutional conflict were declared petty
and insignificant.
The classic conversions were those of Gustav Mevissen and Hermann Baumgarten. After watching the victorious columns march
down Unter den Linden through the Brandenburger Tor, Mevissen,
who had headed the revolutionary cabinet of 1848, described in un-
forgettable words the emotions which gripped him:

> *I cannot shake off the impression of this hour. I am no devotee of Mars;*
> *I feel more attached to the goddess of beauty and the mother of graces*
> *than to the powerful god of war, but the trophies of war exercise a magic*
> *charm upon the child of peace. One's view is involuntarily chained and*
> *one's spirit goes along with the boundless rows of men who acclaim the*
> *god of the moment—success.*

Baumgarten—student of Gervinus, press official of the new era, professor of history at Karlsruhe—remorsefully criticized his earlier convictions in the *Preussische Jahrbücher.* Theoretical and doctrinaire,
the German liberals had placed their faith in words and ideals rather
than in deeds. The middle class was incapable of political leadership. For the solution of its political tasks, he concluded, every people needs the help of an aristocracy.
    With care Bismarck nourished the plant of liberal capitulation.
Soon after the Landtag opened he fed the deputies a series of bills
designed to appeal to every segment of the former opposition. For
men of principle there was a bill of indemnity, for Prussian chauvinists a bill of annexation, for German nationalists a Reichstag
suffrage bill. He appeared in person to defend and explain them
before the committees; in private talks he spun the web of personal
charm and sweet reason which had snared so many diplomatic
opponents. When the situation called for it, the master of scorn and
contempt was equally adept at deference and consideration. He
enjoyed the game intensely. A visitor reported that his face, while
pale and ill, was radiant with laughter. The man was beyond all exaggeration.
    After Königgrätz the liberal deputies were greatly relieved to
learn that the triumphant Junker did not intend a coup against the
constitution and that he was still serious about a national parliament.
Their first chance to respond to his overtures was in the election of

a speaker. Since 1862 Grabow had annually been reelected to that office and his bitter opening speeches had been the first demonstration in each parliamentary session of the continued intransigence of the opposition. But now the deputies chose Forckenbeck, a moderate noted for tact and parliamentary skill. When the reply to the throne speech was drafted, the moderates allowed amendments which made it acceptable even to the conservatives. They argued that the message must demonstrate that the German people were entirely united behind the German policy of the government. Only twenty-five deputies voted against it, including the veteran radical Jacoby, who once more condemned the war as a blow to freedom.

Already there were signs of dissolution in the liberal ranks. In mid-August a left centrist, Kannegiesser, reported to his constituents, "The world-historical events of the last months are having a powerful effect upon men's minds." He detected two currents in both of the major liberal parties: one placed the major emphasis on the German question, the other upon Prussian constitutional law. Relieved of the pressure of the constitutional conflict and presented with the possibility of national unity under authoritarian auspices, the liberal deputies began to divide once more into the two traditional segments of moderate right and democratic left. The unnatural alliance of 1861 broke over the issue of the relative importance of national unity and the rule of law.

Both camps, to be sure, were inclined toward settlement. But the moderates considered the constitutional conflict irretrievably lost and wished to get rid of it on the terms offered by the government, while the democrats were inclined to seek as firm a guarantee as possible for the future respect of parliament's budget rights. The men of the left found it difficult to join the general jubilation. They had not forgotten that the last breach of the constitution—the creation by decree of a system of credit banks—had occurred but two months before the indemnity bill. They noted that even now the minister of Interior continued his "disciplinary" measures against liberal officials and his refusal to confirm liberal city councillors; the minister of justice persisted in his prosecution of the liberal press and opposition deputies (including Twesten). Finally, they observed that the government's indemnity bill contained no guarantee against budgetless rule in the future. When Forckenbeck officially presented the chamber's address, William declared belligerently, "I had to act that way, and I shall do so again, if the same circumstances recur."

In the great debate on the indemnity bill the leaders of the left —Waldeck, Gneist, Ziegler, Virchow, Hoverbeck, Jacoby, Frentzel, and Schulze-Delitzsch—maintained that its passage would legitimize the "gap theory" and pardon four years of unconstitutional behavior on the part of the cabinet. The deputies should postpone the bill pending passage of a legal budget and a law fixing ministerial responsibility. Military victory and respect for law must not be confused with each other. Whatever its successes abroad, the government must stay within the law at home. But the leaders of the right—Twesten, Forckenbeck, Lasker, and Michaelis—feared that, if the liberals remained in opposition, the flight of the voters to the conservatives would continue. By supporting the Bismarck cabinet, on the other hand, they might sever it from its conservative base and influence the future constitutional structure of Germany. In summing up the moderate position, Twesten declared that two issues were fundamental to every state: those of freedom and power. "No one may be criticized for giving precedence to the issue of power at this time and maintaining that the issues of freedom can wait, provided that nothing happens which can permanently prejudice them." From Bismarck the deputies heard of the dangers of French intervention and Austrian resurgence. Only a united people could succeed in Germany's mission against an injured and envious Europe. On September 3 the indemnity bill passed by a vote of 230 to 75.

The constitutional conflict was over, but so also was the unity of the liberal movement. During August and September the caucuses of the Progressive Party became increasingly heated. The exodus of the moderates began with Michaelis, followed by Twesten, Lasker, and many others. By a number of concessions Bismarck gave the secessionists the chance to feel at last the exhilaration of being in harmony with the ruling power. They were permitted to redraft the indemnity bill to make it correspond with the budget clauses of the constitution. Instead of "personal union," Bismarck accepted the actual incorporation of the conquered lands into Prussia, but the introduction of the Prussian constitution was to be delayed one year. A bill presented by Heydt to legalize the government-sponsored credit banks was passed, but only after an amendment which soon put them out of business. A serious clash over the government's request for a credit of sixty million *Thaler* was settled by a compromise which limited the size and purpose of the reserves accumulated by the treasury. Prodded by Lasker and Forckenbeck, the crown issued a general amnesty on September 21, the day of the victory celebration in Berlin. William's request for a donation of one and a half million *Thaler* for the victorious generals was voluntarily amended by the chamber to include the name of Bismarck!

Originally the secessionists did not intend to found a new party. Their aim was to convince the majority of the Left Center and Progressive Parties of the validity of a new strategy. By supporting the Bismarck cabinet in foreign affairs, they hoped to bring it step by step along the road of domestic compromise. But their former comrades remained unconvinced that such a procedure would result in any fundamental changes in the existing order. In the expanded Landtag and constituent Reichstag of 1867 the secessionists found the non-Prussian liberals more sympathetic to their cause. Never personally involved in the Prussian conflict, the latter were untainted by its passions and less concerned about its issues. They too regarded the struggle as lost and relatively unimportant compared to the great task ahead. Out of this union of forces came the National Liberal Party. In numbers the non-Prussians predominated, and the leadership fell to two Hanoverians, Bennigsen and Miquel.

The liberal movement had divided between a Progressive Party, largely Prussian and preserving the tradition of the conflict years, and a National Liberal Party, largely non-Prussian and more national than liberal. To the democratic left the cleavage was between "opportunists" and "men of principle"; to the moderate right it was between "practical statesmen" and "naive idealists." The moderates had taken the road which ultimately led to unconditional surrender, the democrats that which finally ended in frustration and impotence.

Johannes Haller
SIEGFRIED IN POLITICS

As a scholar Johannes Haller was respectable rather than distinguished. He won a reputation in academic circles through his writings on medieval history and his years of teaching at the University of Tübingen. But he exercised his greatest influence as an ardent nationalist attacking the ideals of the Weimar Republic. At a time when democratic institutions in Germany were in desperate need of moral support, he urged his countrymen to find salvation in a strong man like Bismarck who could bring order out of chaos. Before long the savior he was seeking appeared in a brown shirt. Haller lived long enough to see his expectations disappointed as a result of the Second World War. But his views were apparently not altogether discredited, for in 1950 a new edition of his Epochs of German History *was published in Stuttgart.*

It is not always realized what constitutes the actual backbone of a true state. The view is still widely held that the exercise of a constitution, politics in the ordinary acceptance of the term, the activities displayed in parliaments, national assemblies and the like—that these are the mainspring of the nation's political life. This explains the exaggerated importance which is so often attributed to so-called constitutional questions, franchise demands and matters of that sort. Yet one simple reflection is sufficient to show that this view is erroneous, namely, that there have been many states totally lacking in what is generally known as political life which have been by no means negligible. For in reality what today is called politics is only one particular form of the struggle for power in a state. This struggle is always going on, in all ages and in all countries, and will continue to go on, but it takes many different shapes. The actual life of a state may be quite independent of this struggle, for the vital element is the administration, which consists essentially of the body of officials by whom the administration is carried on. Where the civil service or its equivalent remains uninjured, a state can, as history has often demonstrated, survive profound and drastic changes in its constitution, but it is doomed to extinction if its administrative machinery is

From J. Haller, *The Epochs of German History* (London, 1930), pp. 214–215, 220–224, 226–227, 235–239. Reprinted by permission of Routledge & Kegan Paul Ltd.

destroyed, whether by internal dissolution or as the result of external attack.

In Germany's case this backbone of national life—administration, officialdom, call it what you will—was created in the opening decade of the nineteenth century and has lasted up to the present day, sustained the tremendous shock of 1918 and in a large measure lived it down. It is significant to reflect that the elements of disruption, whose *bête noire* is law and order, have always directed their main attacks at this stronghold. . . .

It cannot be too strongly emphasized that all that has been known in Germany for the past hundred years as home politics is not a natural unadulterated product of her own familiar conditions, but has from the very beginning been subject to the influences of foreign models, primarily French and secondarily, and by way of misunderstanding, English—influences which one cannot help calling mischievous and demoralizing.

One of the chief of these was the innovation of a party system. The groups of people with an axe to grind who now began to form parties in Germany, with the object of influencing and reconstructing the state in this way and that according to their various desires, needs, and views, revealed themselves from the very outset as imitations of French models. Their very labels were imported—Conservative, Reactionary, Liberal, Democrat, finally Socialist—nothing but French neologisms. (The fact that some were borrowed by the French from Spain is immaterial.)

Let there be no mistake: this aping of the French has caused untold mischief and confusion, and is still doing so, for the simple reason that a foreign model cannot be arbitrarily imposed on the conditions of another country. For one thing, it suggests the completely erroneous idea that the party system in Germany is just as clear-cut and homogeneous as it is in France. In point of fact, conservatism in southern Germany has never been the same thing as conservatism in the north, while the Democratic Party in the south still has little more than the name in common with its homonym in north Germany. Again, as handed down from the past century *à la française*, Democrat and Conservative should be opposites. Yet in many a little town in Swabia it may be noted that membership of the Democratic Party is by no means inconsistent with an absolutely pig-headed conservatism. And finally, the most pronounced line of division of all, that between different sects, found no place at all in the French paradigm.

The problems, in fact, round which political strife proceeded in Germany in the period following 1815 differed entirely from those of her neighboring country, but the incongruity passed unnoticed, and all with one accord set themselves to imitate the French. In France all the various factions contending for supremacy in the state came from one social stratum, that of the Upper Ten, more especially the moneyed bourgeoisie thrown up by the revolution and the remains of the nobility and leading clergy. In Germany at that time there was, apart from a few exceptional cases, no higher bourgeoisie of this new type. The middle-class element, even including the university intelligentsia from which its leaders came, had not yet, generally speaking, risen above the level of a petty bourgeoisie. It duly assumed the label of liberalism and took up an attitude of opposition to the tutelage of the monarchical, bureaucratic and police régime, but it really had no justification for challenging comparison with the liberalism of France, with which it had nothing in common but the fact of being "agin the government." The struggles of party politics in France at that time were disputes between different shades of the same primary color, like the quarrels of a family over a legacy. In Germany, parties were aligned in opposing camps, since the chief issue was the survival or the abolition of the existing type of government, that of monarchy based on officialdom.

In France parties strove to participate in the government, in Germany to overthrow the government. The French Opposition was quite capable of forming a government, in Germany such a notion was, at all events for some time to come, distinctly remote. Yet the Opposition parties in Germany took the French as their model in all respects. They could only think in French concepts, could only visualize their political ideals in forms which they saw and admired in France. Louis XVIII's celebrated Charter of 1814 represented in the eyes of the majority of a whole generation of Germans the zenith of political achievement and the goal of their own endeavors. It was felt to be imperative that the German states should have a "constitution" *à la française*.

In many cases the governments themselves went half way to meet these demands. From 1818 onwards "constitutions" giving the peoples, through their chosen representatives, a certain share in the responsibilities of government were granted to Weimar, Bavaria, Baden, Hesse-Darmstadt and Württemberg, while the influence of the 1830 revolution in France led to the introduction of similar measures in Hesse-Cassel, Brunswick, Hanover, Oldenburg and Saxony. Thus Germany began to enjoy the benefits of "constitutional government," and the various political groups began to have an opportunity of trying conclusions on the floor of parliaments chosen by popular suffrage.

It is not surprising that at first confusion reigned supreme. Some time had to elapse before men's ideas took definite shape and the various political tendencies were clearly differentiated one from another. The Democrats were all for setting up republics in which the ideals of *Liberté*, *Egalité*, and *Fraternité* should be put into practice. The Liberals were different; they wanted limited monarchies with Houses of Parliament on the English model, such as had recently been introduced in France and Belgium. But all of them looked to foreign countries for their political instruction and inspiration. For one set, Great Britain was the paragon of states; for the other Paris was "Freedom's Mecca." Whenever native politicians in Germany held forth on freedom and the rights of the people, one could be quite sure that they were largely repeating what they had been reading in the French newspapers. Others, again, conceived a grand passion for Poland, another fighter for "liberty." They did not grasp that hers was a case which presented an entirely different problem, namely, that of the self-determination of one nationality at grips with another—a problem to which there was no parallel in contemporary Germany. But no! Liberty was Liberty. This most ill-used of words could act like a charm on the mind of any shopkeeper in Baden or the Palatinate who nursed a grievance against his prince over some detail in the local police regulations, until he would see in the Polish nobleman in rebellion against the domination of the Tsar of Russia a companion in distress, a brother and a comrade in arms, fighting under the same banner. This was the classic age of xenomania in Germany, an affliction which found characteristic expression at a Festival of Freedom held at Hambach in the Palatinate in 1832, when the Polish flag was displayed side by side with the German colors and one of the speakers called for cheers for the three sister nations, Germany, France and Poland—Germany, forsooth, hobnobbing with her two deadly enemies!

But we of the present generation have forfeited the right to pass judgment over-strictly on such aberrations as these. The Germany of today has fallen into far graver error, without even the excuse of ignorance, which was a valid one a century ago. The people who displayed that absurd enthusiasm for foreigners and their methods of government had had no political experience. Their procedure in developing their constitutional theories was much the same as that of the typical German in Heine's story, who could draw a camel without having ever set eye upon such an animal: they turned their eyes inwards and painted the ideal picture of the state of the world as it appeared in the depths of their sentimental imaginations. Most of them had never visited the foreign countries whom they were proposing to adopt as mentors. They went on singing the praises of English, French or Belgian legislation without the remotest idea of the real situation in those countries; few suspected that it was very different from the conception formed of it in Germany.

That was the curse of German political life from the outset, that while it moved within the limited spheres of petty states, and petty bourgeois mentality, it constantly aimed at imitating the ways of the larger, homogeneous nations. This was the reason for the sterility of those early decades of German parliamentary life, which might otherwise have been of so much value as a training for the nation's political capacity. None of the parliaments at Munich, Stuttgart, Karlsruhe or elsewhere provided any real education in political method, even for the most zealous of students, for the simple reason that no real political life existed in any of the states. . . .

In fact, the whole marshalled forces of actuality were pressing in the direction of unity. Political unification was not a romantic dream of youthful idealists, but a necessity of everyday life. It had to come, in fact it seemed to be coming as it were of its own momentum, especially since the Zollverein had largely succeeded in unifying the system of communication throughout Germany. As early as 1840 a French observer travelling through Germany gained the clear impression that unity was being reestablished. "What a magnificent spectacle," he wrote, "it is to see a great people drawing together the scattered fragments of its heritage, recreating a sentiment of nationality, and, as it were, entering into full life again!"

Yet this unity could not be achieved without effort. The idea might go on ripening, the force of public opinion in its favor might gather strength, but before it could be turned into reality, a creative act of will was required, and this must come from one definite source. It became more and more clear that this source could be none other than Prussia. In spite of all the criticism levelled against the Prussian government from all parts of Germany, Prussia was recognized more and more widely as the destined deliverer of the nation from the morass of impotent pettiness into which it had fallen. There was simply no other possible way of salvation; the stern logic of facts pointed to that solution only. Edgar Quinet, who knew Germany well and sensed the vast secret longing of her heart, realized this as early as 1832, and was alive to the danger which threatened his own country. He warned his compatriots prophetically: "Prussia will bring forth a Man! . . ."

To all appearances it had been demonstrated that Germany was unable to win her way to unity. Necessary as unity was to her, passionately as she desired it, it seemed impossible, impracticable. The rulers were unwilling, the people unable to bring it into being. The best minds in the nation relapsed into dull dejection, their sole remaining hope lying in a miracle, a hero who might make his appearance and unify Germany as if by magic. From many a heart all over the country during those gloomy years the cry went up for a Hero— a Great Man who would heal all divisions by the magic power of his genius and with a grip of iron would force all Germany—princes and people alike—to join together in unity. In tones of longing the Swabian poet Fischer thus apostrophized this savior yet unknown:

> *Hero, if thou be living at this hour,*
> *Arise, we rest our hopes and faith in thee!*
> *What if it be Dictatorship thou bringest,*
> *Thrice welcome thou, Dictator of the Free!*

And he came, he arose and accomplished the task as the poets demanded. The strong wise dictator imposed his will on the whole world. In this one instance Fate smiled on the German nation, which had so often tasted the bitterness of her displeasure, seen so many buds crushed and so many blossoms broken before the fruit could form, been so often deprived of leadership. At this juncture the right man really did appear at the right moment.

The structure, the foundation of which was laid by the genius of Frederick the Great but which had been left untouched by his successors, and the completion of which was desired with ever increasing intensity by three generations of Germans, who yet could not discover the way to accomplish it, was brought to a triumphant finish by the genius of Bismarck in eight short years. The problem which seemed as baffling as the squaring of the circle was solved, and the solution was as simple, as unerring and as elegant as Columbus' famous trick with the egg.

Bismarck was no conjurer, no miracle-worker, but his mind was a magic mirror which showed him the reality of things as they were. He realized that German unity could only be attained if the duel which had started in 1740 were fought out to a decisive result. For three generations this awkward fact had been overlooked or burked, but Bismarck saw to it that the truth should prevail. He knew that only the old Prussian spirit, the Prussia of Frederick the Great, could solve the problem. His contemporaries imagined that force was no longer necessary, and that a general profession of faith in the new Liberal ideals must of itself lead to the unification of Germany under the Prussian banner. Bismarck dispelled this fog of well-meaning self-deception with word and deed. His new message rang out: Not by speeches or by passing resolutions, but by blood and iron! He realized in addition what had been so entirely lost sight of in the Frankfurt deliberations, that the German constitution was a matter of European importance, and that only by an extraordinarily favorable conjunction of circumstances could the German people hope to decide their own fate without foreign intervention. In 1848 the opportunity had been there, but it had been allowed to pass by unused. Bismarck watched for its recurrence, and the moment he saw the other European Powers at loggerheads and unable to take joint action, he struck.

He was the right man in the right place, equipped with every quality which his task required: an experienced parliamentarian, a professional diplomatist, Conservative but without prejudices, Ger-

man and Prussian combined, strong and subtle, bold and shrewd—
a man to be trusted. And every possible obstacle was placed in his
way. He was opposed, hated, despised and vilified, and only a merci-
ful fate spared him from falling a victim to an assassin's bullet at the
most critical moment. The nation did not recognize her savior, would,
in fact, willingly have crucified him or burned him alive. He had to
save his country as he once saved a groom from drowning, by gripping it by the throat. When he had won and the work was practically
over, then they cheered and lauded him to the skies. But what was
the value of such belated converts? From the vast majority of the
nation there never came a spark of understanding for the statesman
who gave them what they wanted but had been incapable of obtaining themselves. As for learning from his wisdom, they obstinately
refused to do anything of the sort.

This is not the place to dwell on his achievements. What is rele-
vant to our discussion is common knowledge, and I am relieved not
to have to enter into it in detail. For I must confess that I cannot
utter the name of Bismarck without a sense of shame. I cannot help
feeling how applicable to him are the lines in which a Swabian poet
and patriot ninety years ago addressed the spirit of the national hero,
Arminius:

> *Legend tells that fallen heroes wander*
> *Ghost-like till mankind their message heeds.*
> *Still must thou be restless, still rebellious,*
> *In a world which stultifies thy deeds.*

The Bismarck celebrations which are constantly being held nowadays
strike me as almost of the nature of blasphemy. What right have the
men of this generation to celebrate Bismarck's glory, when they have
done worse than kill him, have abandoned the structure he built to
decay and ruin?

When his work was completed the world imagined that Germany
had turned her back on the past and begun a new and splendid page
in her history—a period of fulfillment and happiness after such long
years of waiting and suffering. Looking back as we are able to do
now, we are constrained to say that that was a mistake. Bismarck's
creation contained potentialities of a new era, but the generation that

followed him was unable to turn these potentialities to account. Germany forgot all too quickly that what she had inherited from Bismarck was a sacred trust, a fiduciary legacy subject to the condition that the capital should be maintained intact and unhypothecated—in other words, that the price of security was eternal vigilance. Instead of proving worthy of this trust and expanding to the measure of his design, the nation clung to its old errors and closed its ears to the claims of loyalty and gratitude. The German Empire which Bismarck founded turned out to be a mere episode, a temporary break in the continuity of seven centuries in which the years 1648 and 1815 are the notable dates and 1918 their worthy congener.

One's reflections inevitably take this tinge in the atmosphere of today, and our study must end on a harsh discord; or, rather, it does not end, but merely points in dumb emotion to an unseen future.

We are all aware that Germany was never stricken so low as she is today. It is difficult not to despair and accept as the verdict of history the Biblical *Mene, Tekel, Upharsin.*

And yet something fundamental, a vital instinct, tells us that this verdict cannot be final, while our knowledge of the past history of the nation authorizes us to enter a *caveat* against the precipitate judgments of the passing hour. More than once in the past it has seemed as though Germany were lost beyond all human hope. Think of 1648, of 1808! But again and again the stubborn vitality and sterling qualities of her people have restored her, after painful exertion, to life and a more propitious future. Can this nation have lost its power of recovery? It is for the present generation to show that the same qualities are still at the nation's disposal, essentially unimpaired, and capable of renewed and vigorous effort. The fall may have been greater this time, but that was partly due to the fact that the height attained was also greater than ever before. Why should the nation not be able to cherish hopes of a fresh revival? History may demonstrate once more, as it did a century ago, that great events which seem at the time to have happened in vain bear fruit in later years. Then it was memories of the War of Liberation, now it may be the memory of the Bismarck era and the fleeting glories of the age he rendered possible that will fructify and bring forth a rich harvest at the appointed time. It will depend upon our own endeavors. If we Germans do our duty, we are justified in looking to the future with faith in our hearts.

He who listens to the voice of history will hear the words of promise echoing down the centuries:

We bid you hope!

Erich Eyck
THE SUBVERTER OF FREEDOM

The most important revisionist biography of Bismarck appeared appropriately enough during the Second World War. Its author was Erich Eyck, a German lawyer and historian who was forced to seek refuge in England from persecution by the National Socialists. An admirer of the British liberal tradition, he condemned the Iron Chancellor for stifling the growth of representative institutions in Central Europe. He was sharply attacked by those historians among whom the Bismarck cult is still strong. But his work is on the whole a healthy antidote to the hero worship usually accorded the unifier of Germany. The selection which follows describes the period of constitutional conflict in Prussia which began in 1862.

Bismarck's appointment made a great but on the whole a very unfavorable impression. The London *Spectator* called him the most outspoken Junker who had ever ruled in Prussia, and a man of strong but limited understanding. The German, and particularly the Prussian, Liberals felt that a great struggle was ahead. One of the leaders of the Progressive Party wrote:

> *Bismarck, that is to say: government without budget, rule by the sword in home affairs, and war in foreign affairs. I consider him the most dangerous minister for Prussia's liberty and happiness.*

This expressed the popular feeling rather accurately. In the theaters, every malicious allusion to the king was received with a storm of applause.

Bismarck's first task was to form his cabinet. The foreign minister,

From Erich Eyck, *Bismarck and the German Empire*, 2nd ed. (London, 1958), pp. 58–63. Copyright 1958 by George Allen & Unwin Ltd. Reprinted by permission of The Macmillan Company and George Allen & Unwin Ltd.

Count Bernstorff, and the minister of finance, von der Heydt, again declined to govern unconstitutionally without a budget and retired from the government. At first Bismarck tried to make contact with moderate Liberals. For instance, he asked Twesten, the mover of the compromise amendment, to see him. Bismarck did not have strong views about the length of military service. For his own person he would have accepted the two years' period; but as the king was opposed to it there was nothing he was able to offer to Twesten. So the interview came to nothing. It is remarkable, anyhow, for the rather startling and indiscreet way in which Bismarck talked to this member of the Opposition about the king who just had appointed him. He compared the king with a horse that shied at every new object and became restive and unmanageable if one tried force, but would get accustomed to it little by little.

Bismarck never had the serious intention of taking a Liberal into his cabinet. As a matter of fact, he composed it of reactionary officials who had no other merit than their conservative opinions and their noble birth. In later years Bismarck spoke of most of them in the most depreciating and disdainful way. The finance minister, von Bodelschwingh, he calls "a liar," and the agricultural minister, von Selchow, an ass (*Rindvieh*). Only the minister of the interior, Graf Eulenburg, was a man of gifts, though idle and frivolous. However insignificant these Junkers were, they met the two requirements for which Bismarck wanted ministers: they were all ready to help him to crush the Opposition and to let him make his foreign policy without putting any obstacles in his way.

In parliament, Bismarck began his activities by withdrawing the budget for the next year. Asked in the committee of the House what he proposed to do next, he made a speech which caused the greatest sensation. He took from his pocketbook an olive-branch—it was the olive-branch Katherine Orloff had given him when they parted in Avignon—showed it to the members of the committee with the words that it had been his intention to offer it to the House as a token of peace, but that he had now reluctantly come to the conclusion that it was still too early. He then spoke about Prussia's present situation and future task. Germany did not look, he said, to the liberalism of Prussia but to her power. Unfortunately, her frontiers were unfavorable to a healthy state. The great questions of the time could not be solved by speeches and majority votes—that was the great mistake of 1848 and 1849—but by *blood and iron.*

The sensation these startling sentences made was the very reverse of favorable. Even Roon grew angry about these "racy excursions," which did not help in any way. The historian Heinrich von Treitschke, later the most outspoken prophet of Bismarck, raged about the ridiculous vulgarity of this shallow Junker boasting of the blood and iron with which he wanted to subjugate Germany. The king was not gratified either. He was in Baden at the time in the company of the queen, their daughter, the grand duchess of Baden, and their son-in-law, the grand duke. Bismarck knew that none of them was his friend, and he was afraid that they would turn his words against him. To win back the king, he met him in the train at the last station before Berlin, Jüterbog. Of this episode Bismarck has given a masterly description in his *Recollections* (chapter 12).

Whatever the king may have thought about Bismarck's utterances, he knew that he was indispensable for dealing with the chamber. In the great debate which arose there, and in which moderate and radical members alike refuted Bismarck's constitutional arguments, one of the moderate speakers, the famous lawyer, Professor Gneist, emphasized the point of principle. He warned the minister to respect an elementary quality of the German people: its belief in a firm moral and legal order as the last and decisive factor in the history of states. Gneist was right. Such was then, indeed, the feeling of the most important section of the Prussian people. The great question was whether this belief in the decisive power of the legal and moral order would be justified by events.

At first, developments took quite the opposite turn. The budget voted by the Chamber of Deputies was thrown out by the feudal Chamber of Seigneurs (Herrenhaus) and the government ruled without a budget. It continued to collect taxes and duties and to spend the collected money for military purposes quite arbitrarily. As it was a period of flourishing economic life, the yield of the taxes increased, so that the government was not embarrassed owing to want of money. The chamber was unable to stop this process. It lacked the legal means either to stop the collection of the taxes or to impeach the government. The constitution declared that the ministers were responsible, but it did not open a way for their impeachment if they broke the constitution. Therefore, the power of the Chamber of Deputies was weak. Foreign critics failed to understand this position. English journals, for instance, often ascribed to lack of firmness in the Opposition what was, in fact, a weakness in its constitutional power.

How deeply Bismarck's methods offended the sense of justice of the German people came to light in the debate of the Chamber of Deputies on the address in January 1863. The official speaker of the committee of the House was the famous historian, Heinrich von Sybel, the same historian who under the auspices of Bismarck afterwards wrote his *History of the Foundation of the German Empire by William I.* He was not at all a radical, but a warm admirer of Prussia and her history. Sybel said:

> *The Ministers and the majority of this House speak a different language; their thoughts are ruled by a different logic and their actions by different moral laws.*

But the climax of the debate came when Bismarck bluntly told the House:

> *If a compromise cannot be arrived at and a conflict arises, then the conflict becomes a question of power. Whoever has the power, then acts according to his opinion.*

It was not a radical but the moderate Count Schwerin, a former minister of King William during the "New Era," who answered with these words:

> *The sentence in which the speech of the Prime Minister culminated: that "Might before Right," that "you may talk as you like, we have the power and will therefore force through our theory"—this is not a sentence which can support the dynasty of Prussia in the long run. The sentence on which the greatness of our dynasty and of our country rests, and the reverence which Prussia's sovereigns have enjoyed and will enjoy for ever and ever, is quite the reverse: "Right before Might."*

These words made a deep impression, and Count Schwerin was hailed as the defender of the good old Prussian tradition.

Bismarck defied the chamber, as the young William Pitt, in 1783, defied Charles Fox and the majority of the House of Commons. Both relied on their king. But there was a very important difference. Pitt knew that the voters, or those who directed the voters, were on his side, that he only had to bide his time to dissolve parliament in order to get a favorable majority. Bismarck knew that the people were even more passionately against him than the chamber. Time and again he dissolved the chamber: the voters always elected the same majority. All the vehement and often illegal pressure of the government did not succeed in making them vote for governmental candidates. The Prussian Opposition in the years 1862–1866 is, indeed, the only one in the whole history of constitutional Germany which could effectively depend upon their voters. In later years, 1878, 1887, 1893, 1907, a dissolution always gave the government the majority it wanted, because enough voters deserted the oppositional deputies. Only in the time of the Prussian constitutional conflict did they stick invariably to their guns. True, they voted according to the three-classes-suffrage, and the middle-class voters of the two first classes decided the election. But there can be no doubt that the majority of the workers in the third class sympathized fully with them. . . .

A government that encroaches on the constitution at one point, cannot stop there. It is forced by circumstances and by its own action from one illegality to another. The next point of attack was the freedom of the press, guaranteed by the constitution. The great majority of the newspapers was Liberal and supported the Opposition energetically. Bismarck tried to suppress them by an order of the king in June 1863, which empowered the police to suppress oppositional papers. By dissolving the chamber he managed to silence the press during the election. Nevertheless, the Opposition was again victorious at the polls and the order had to be cancelled after having been in force for five months.

This royal order against the press had a startling effect in an unexpected quarter. The heir to the throne, the crown prince, openly declared his opposition to it. The crown prince and his wife, Victoria, did not by any means approve of Bismarck's methods. They objected to his encroachments on the constitution and were afraid that they would open an insuperable gulf between the Prussian people and the dynasty. The prince warned the king against a breach of the constitution. The king had ordered him to attend the councils when he himself presided (*Kronrat*). But the decision to make the royal order against the press had been made when the prince was absent. He was on a tour of military inspection in the eastern provinces of the monarchy, when he suddenly learnt of the order for the first time by its publication in the press. On the advice of Princess Victoria, who accompanied him, and of the Liberal Chief Burgomaster of Danzig, Winter, he declared, answering a speech by Winter in the Danzig Town Hall: "I did not know anything of this order beforehand. I was absent. I am not one of those who advised it."

These words inevitably caused a tremendous sensation. The Prussian people was deeply moved by the open opposition of the heir to the throne; the king, on the other hand, was extremely angry and wrote his son a furious letter treating him, as Victoria wrote to her mother, like a little child. Victoria's letters, published by Sir Frederick Ponsonby in the *Letters of the Empress Frederick* and partly in the Second Series of the *Letters of Queen Victoria*, show the immensely difficult position in which the crown prince and his wife then found themselves. The Danzig episode became a decisive event in their lives. Bismarck never either forgot or forgave this opposition. Thus began the isolation of the princely couple, which from that time onwards cast a shadow over their lives. Bismarck's own point of view is given in his correspondence with the king, published in chapter 16 of *Reflections and Recollections*. His marginal notes on the memorandum of the prince state his case in a masterly manner. He based his arguments on the thesis that a crown prince did not have any official "status" and was therefore not entitled to play a political rôle and to make opposition to his father. But what would Bismarck himself have done if he had had a king whose policy he disliked, and a crown prince who supported him—in other words, if Frederick III had come to the throne, not struck down by his terrible and mortal malady but in full strength, and if his reign had lasted longer than merely ninety-nine short days? Fate has spared Bismarck this test. But whoever knows the story of those tragic ninety-nine days of 1888 will doubt whether Bismarck would have acted according to his doctrine of 1863.

III UNIFIER OF GERMANY

Heinrich von Srbik
THE AUSTRIAN TRAGEDY

The decline and fall of the Austrian Empire haunted Heinrich von Srbik all his life. Contemplating the tragic destiny of his country, he came to the conclusion that its mission had been to uphold the supranational unity of Central Europe. In a series of important works he portrayed the Habsburg state as the last stronghold of the universalist tradition of the Middle Ages. His greatest book, Deutsche Einheit: Idee und Wirklichkeit, *deals with the Austro-Prussian conflict in the nineteenth century. In the following selection Srbik analyzes in his involved, turgid prose the consequences of the Hohenzollern victory of 1866.*

In that year the forces of the German past were engaged in a struggle with the youthful forces of German growth regarding the form of German national life. This struggle involved the immanent vital laws of the state; it involved the multiformity of the German spirit arising out of the multiformity of the German body politic, engaged in conflict with the youthful German spirit reflecting the civic unity of the national community. The law of all existence is also valid for the vital political form of great peoples and nations conscious of their destiny. The structure of political existence was and is shaped by creative forces which embody principles and determine appropriate political forms and the nature of law. They lead a life of their own consistent with their time. As long as they possess the capacity for inspiring action, their form and law have a higher justification. But then opposing forces arise, pulsating with a more vigorous life, which demand a new political form and a new law, which triumphantly drive the old powers to exhaustion and death. The unifying and relatively eternal element in the evolution of civic and political forms is the great nation, bound by ties of blood and spirit to a unique organic essence, intimately connected with a geographic area, unfolding its potentialities. Out of the interrelationship of independent nations arises the community of peoples which we call humanity, the world, and Europe. The deed acts as a motive force, reinforcing

From Heinrich von Srbik, *Deutsche Einheit: Idee und Wirklichkeit vom Heiligen Reich bis Königgrätz,* 4 vols. (Munich, 1935–1942), IV: 463–469. Reprinted by permission of F. Bruckmann K. G. Verlag. Translated by Theodore S. Hamerow and William W. Beyer.

the energies which create a new order among peoples. But not everything which falls victim, which becomes the past is doomed to death
as soon as the new form of life becomes reality thanks to its youthful vigor and its conscious, willful deed.

If we regard the course of German history from this point of view,
then we can no longer treat with the usual scorn the many centuries
of the first German Empire, the half century of the German Confederation, and the former leading role of Austria in Germany. The aged
Holy Roman Empire had at one time lived a life of immeasurable
greatness. It died not only through external violence, but through
the enfeeblement of an idea embracing and unifying the whole, an
idea exercising effective power. The German Confederation, which
owed its origins to historic tendencies arising out of the past, which
was in many respects the spiritual and political if not the legal heir
of the empire, had to perish when the form and the law of the past
came into irreconcilable conflict with the living law of the present
demanding a new order of things. Such also was the fate of the
primacy in German affairs of Austria, the old wearer of the imperial
crown, who represented on a reduced scale the faded idea of empire, and who predominated in the German Confederation. And such
was the fate of the second German Empire, when in the absence of
inspiring goals and of a true, profound conception of the nation, its
vital inner energies turned to an overemphasis on material gain and
to spiritual discord. External and internal causes always joined in the
downfall of the old order, while profound needs and great accomplishments always led to a new act of creation. . . .

In this sense we can clearly comprehend the national and world
significance of the year 1866. . . . The German people as an organism required by virtue of its inner law of life a new political order
which could secure for it life-giving unity at home and a position of
political power in the world in keeping with its greatness. The structure of the German Confederation under the primacy of Austria could
no longer satisfy this requirement. Both were too greatly encumbered
with the heritage of ideas and forms, with the traditions of centuries
to be able to create a vigorous new Germany. As long as the
sovereignty of the individual German states in diplomatic and military affairs was not willingly or unwillingly surrendered in favor of the
sovereignty of a federal government representing the political inter-

ests of the nation, as long as the dualism of two great powers divided Germany, a sound solution of the German problem in the foreseeable future was inconceivable. This German dualism in turn endowed the idea of trialism with a certain vitality. The subordination of one power to the other was an impossibility, since neither Prussia nor Austria could accept the leadership of her opponent. The only alternatives were the curtailment of the power of one of the two great states to the point of its absorption into a greater Germany led by its rival, or the exclusion of one of the two great states, in other words, a smaller Germany. The separation of Prussia from the German body politic was something which the purely Prussian outlook of King William could at times consider a necessity. This was never true of Bismarck, however, who acted out of Prussian state interest, but maintained that Prussian and German interests were concurrent. The exclusion of Austria from Germany was something which a particularistic Austrian outlook could accept, but this was never true of a German national will directed toward all of the German people and toward Central Europe. The division split the nation down the middle. Austria at that time could not find a way and purpose capable of solving her own problems of organization, while in the vital German question she also found herself in a state of indecision, caught between the demands of an old, dying order and a maturing new epoch. She clung to a formal legality, yet Bismarck and the Prussian state smashed that legality. They became the great destroyers of the inclusive German Confederation, just as once Prussia had grown great at the expense of the Holy Roman Empire, contributing significantly to its collapse through Frederick the Great. But both of them, the creative political genius and his state, offered non-Austrian Germany something which Austria could not offer: a vital order, the unity of will and action of the majority of the people. Here was their higher historical function in Germany, here was their higher legality vis-à-vis Austria.

This function and legality strengthened them also in dealing with the world of the middle and small states of Germany, the most loyal advocates besides Austria of the associative, federative principle. In honor of the German past let it be said once more that even in the old inclusive outlook of this third Germany there was a great deal of strong German consciousness and genuine love for the entire nation, along with particularism and separatism of various sorts. But the reform from which even many members of the Diet of the Confederation hopefully expected a revival of German power and German spirit was thwarted not only by the opposition of Prussia, but also by the nature of the confederation itself, by the irreconcilable divisions within the third group of states, by the inability to satisfy the vital claim of the nation to a truly new form of existence establishing federal unity and freedom for all of Germany. Yet it was precisely this goal which Bismarck attained by the revolution from above, in opposition to the majority of the German and the Prussian people. The dream which he had dreamed early in 1863, at a time of great strain, became reality. In that dream he is riding up a narrow Alpine path, an abyss on the right, cliffs to the left. And then the horse refuses to go on. It is impossible to turn around or dismount. With the whip which he is holding in his left hand he strikes the smooth wall of the rock and calls on God. The whip begins to extend, and the wall of the rock slides away like scenery on a stage, opening a broad passage with a view of hills and forests like those of Bohemia, revealing Prussian troops and banners.

The architect of the second German Empire never became an advocate of a greater Germany including Austria. But even the "striving for Germany" in the form of a smaller empire was not as yet apparent in his peace negotiations of 1866. He who had approached and solved the German problem always keeping in mind its European context could not as yet consider at Nikolsburg and Prague his second objective, the national unification of Germany under Prussian hegemony without Austria, because of the other Great Powers. Did not France for reasons of "security" demand Bavarian and Hessian territory left of the Rhine, including the fortress of Mainz, Luxemburg, and Limburg? Did not Bismarck need the support of Russia, whose fear of a revolution in Poland grew as soon as the victor incited revolution in the Danubian monarchy, who looked with disfavor on any serious weakening of Austria, on the extensive Prussian annexations, on the dethronement of dynasties? Her tsar hoped for the joint intervention of the neutral Great Powers, urging the convocation of a congress. It was because of the tsar that Bismarck had to spare the south German states and leave Oberhessen to the grand duchy. He spared Saxony in deference to Austria, content to persuade his king to approve the complete annexation of Hanover and Hesse-Kassel which aroused only platonic feelings in England and Russia. His design did not extend beyond what could be safely attained. On August 1, 1866, he wrote to his son Wilhelm: "What we need is north Germany, and that is where we want to expand." In the new organization of Germany he allowed the south German states to remain politically independent side by side with the North German Confederation. But he crossed the boundary of the Main River by means of defensive and offensive alliances. The future might bring "opportunity and luck." A new empire was seen by Bismarck in 1866 as only a desirable possibility, yet that same year also opened the way for its realization.

What died at Königgrätz was not only the old empire which, as has already often been pointed out, had found a continuation of its ideal in the German Confederation; the old Central Europe and the old Europe also died. The famous exclamation of the Papal Secretary of State Cardinal Antonelli, *"Casca il mondo, Casca il mondo,"* expressed the truth. Now that a strong Germany under strong leadership had arisen, even if not as yet in the form of a legally organized political community, the position of France as arbiter and hegemon of the Continent, the result and bulwark of German disunity, was destined to end. It was no longer possible for the neighboring power to divide Germany in two at the most vulnerable point in the west, in the most vital region of the old German Empire. "Germany's misfortune," to use the phrase of Edmund Jörg, was now at an end, the misfortune "that we in Germany support one and a half million soldiers in our budgets, and yet must tremble at every frown of the imperator." With Austria, the empire, and the confederation fell also the remnants of the old universalist, political connection of the German nation to Rome.

With good reason did Pope Pius IX in 1860 insert the name of the emperor of Austria in place of the *Imperator Romanorum* in the liturgical prayer on Good Friday. With good reason did he say at the beginning of the year of decision: "There are only two sovereigns who defend the eternal principles on which thrones rest, Emperor Francis Joseph and I." While the residence city of the Romano-German emperors for long centuries, the capital of the Austrian imperial state, was being threatened by the Prussian army columns, while the Diet of the German Confederation was fleeing as the Prussian regiments marched into the free city on the Main, an English diplomat spoke of the end of the indirect universal rule of Austria which had extended from the Eider to Brindisi, he spoke of the destruction for all time of the Austrian dream of the Holy Roman Empire. Prussia achieved the victory of the national over the universal principle not only in German national life, but for the Italian nation as well. Without Prussia and Bismarck, Italy would not have attained what was essentially the completion of her national unification. The evacuation of the fortresses of the Quadrilateral, the transfer of Venetia to Napoleon and by him to Victor Emmanuel—how could the state vanquished at Custozza and Lissa have won these prizes without Königgrätz? And on July 3, 1866, the temporal rule of the pope over Rome and the *Patrimonium Petri* suffered what was to prove a fatal blow, until the third of the wars of German unification destroyed it completely.

The higher law of life and death decreed that twelve million Germans in Austria should become the victims of the partial unity which was the good fortune of a great majority of the nation. The period of Austria's leadership in the great German commonwealth would not have come to an end in 1866 without Bismarck, but it could not have continued much longer in any event. A great people conscious of its right to life would have sooner or later, peacefully or by force, rejected all artificial political forms as a matter of inner necessity. It would have rejected the primacy of a triumphant Austria in a new confederation including a weakened Prussia and strengthened middle states, a confederation which might represent the proper geographic boundaries, but not the true civic unity of the nation. It would have rejected a division of Germany into a northern confederation under Prussian and a southern confederation under Austrian leadership, for such an arrangement, as Kübeck says, could not have permanently suppressed the yearning of the nation "to build again a whole state out of the two half Germanys." It would have rejected the trialistic fantasies of the passionately patriotic Hermann Orges, who envisioned a "purely German" confederation under the presidency of the emperor of Austria, and then perhaps in the distant future the emergence of a "higher confederation" including both large states. The withdrawal of the German element of Austria from the German body politic was the result of a terrible operation, which by amputating a limb brought new strength and rich development to a sick body.

Never again could the old, lax, inclusive system be revived, as Francis Joseph hoped in the first years after Königgrätz.

The historical thought and sentiment of the old advocates of a greater German commonwealth could not comprehend that the bonds which had endured for a millennium were broken. They saw only violence, perfidy, and illegality at work, failing to recognize the profound causes of change. While the political Catholics stood mourning at the grave of their Catholic *grossdeutsch* world and their dream of a Catholic empire, they also felt a genuine, national grief at the loss of their German brothers in Austria. They shared the spirit of Biegeleben's angry sonnets. Königgrätz and its political consequences also produced a sense of deep shock among the liberal protagonists of a *grossdeutsch* state. There is, for example, the gripping poem "Königgrätz" by the Hessian democrat Adam Trabert, in which a German Austrian wounded by a Prussian bullet cries out in anguish: "I lie here deep in clover, slain by my German brethren." Besides burning grief at the separation of German Austria from the nation as a whole, there was in German hearts on both sides of the new frontier bleak pessimism about Austria's future and despair concerning the fate of the separated part of the nation.

Hermann Oncken

GALLIC AMBITION

In his scholarship Hermann Oncken belonged to the Rankean tradition. He believed that the historian must judge calmly and dispassionately, without rancor or patriotic zeal. But in his treatment of French diplomacy during the 1860s he could not suppress a national pride which was intensified by Germany's humiliation at Versailles in 1919. His study of Napoleon III and the Rhine was based on thorough research, but there can be no mistaking the villain of the piece. Whether embodied in Louis Napoleon or Raymond Poincaré, Gallic ambition leads inexorably to war.

From Hermann Oncken, *Napoleon III and the Rhine: The Origin of the War of 1870–1871* (New York: Alfred A. Knopf, Inc., 1928), pp. 183–194.

With soldierly frankness the French military attaché in Berlin, Colonel Stoffel, discussed the true cause of the war at the time of its outbreak. He said that the war was the result of the preponderance of Prussia since 1866 and that this preponderance required France to secure her boundaries. Such security, he felt, she could attain only by acquiring the German territory west of the Rhine, and French possession of the Rhine alone could guarantee the peace between the two nations. These utterances are in agreement with the facts as we have revealed them according to the documents, except that the documents go even further and show that already prior to the war of 1866 Napoleon had a Rhine policy and by an unsuccessful intrigue had himself helped to establish the order which later he believed he could subvert only by conquering the Rhine. This is corroborated by the fact that as late as August 6, the day of the battle of Wörth, Prince Metternich, who had a deeper insight than anyone else into the Napoleonic policies of 1863–1870, spoke outright of the Rhine as the chief war aim. This fact, usually kept dark in France nowadays, was emphasized on September 18, 1919, by the French socialist J. Longuet in a parliamentary address, when he said that it should not be forgotten that the yearning for the left bank of the Rhine was responsible for the war of 1870.

In July 1870, to be sure, French diplomacy had to speak a quite different language abroad. The louder the rabble in Paris clamored for the Rhine, the more zealously did France try to make the outside world believe that she was waging no war of aggression. Although there was little enough serious hope of winning over the south German states, the French government, in all declarations made prior to the final decision of south Germany, made a particular point of stating that it did not intend to take an inch of German soil and wished merely to check the further growth of Prussia. Gramont even went so far as expressly to disavow to the Bavarian minister the demands for the Rhine voiced by the Paris press and was careful to have this noble renunciation loudly proclaimed especially in the Viennese press, so that public sentiment in German Austria might not be estranged but might be prepared for a war on the side of France.

But did these formal declarations, which culminated in Napoleon's war manifesto of July 23, contain the whole truth, or did they admit of evasion and doubtful interpretation? It has already been mentioned that Denmark was to receive as the minimum price of her cooperation all of Schleswig—in other words territory of distinctly German stamp which had been hotly contested for a generation. And what the French were prepared to offer Austria in the event of cooperation, is clear from the negotiations carried on ever since 1866. There can be no doubt that in case of victory not only Silesia would have changed hands; it is more than likely that the old Austrian craving for Bavarian territory would have cropped up again too. And what of the specifically French war objectives?

While publicly stressing nonannexation, Paris found it necessary to resort once more to the substitute for pure annexation which it had for years advocated as a solution compatible with German self-respect and national consciousness, and sugared with so many secret hopes. The autonomous Rhineland state appears once more as a French war aim in the decisive hour. At any rate the French minister in Stuttgart allowed this rather obscure remark to escape him:

> *according to the plans made in Paris in the last few years it is the French aim, in case of victory, to establish a state of about five million inhabitants along the Rhine, perhaps for the King of Hanover.*

Gramont too spoke to the Bavarian minister of a restoration and enlargement of Hanover in order to destroy the Prussian preponderance. Although he considered it more expedient not to mention the Rhineland state expressly, he revealed his intention in another way by hinting at the "annulment" of Baden as a Prussian subsidiary. It will be remembered that it was Gramont too who as early as April 1867, had offered the Austrians south Germany as far as the Black Forest and had shown a special French interest only for Baden. These few points will suffice to disclose the extent of French "renunciation" with respect to German soil. In reverting to the old idea of a neutral state along the Rhine, as a policy which ought to prove acceptable to Europe, France realized of course that in case the treaty of peace were really dictated in Berlin, this modest policy, which was always considered a minimum requirement, would not have to stand.

But the French revealed not only individual phases of their war program. At one point they developed the program in its entirety, though in a discreet form. We refer to the declaration which Gramont early in August was indiscreet enough to make to the Russian chargé in official form, describing it expressly as containing the minimum demands of France. This list includes annexation pure and simple. In demanding the cession of the Saar basin Gramont clearly violated the solemn promise not to claim even a bit of German territory. As for the boundaries in 1814, which ever since 1860 were regarded as the most modest satisfaction of French needs, French diplomacy was accustomed to regard them as resting on an old legal title. But the sum total of the German territorial modifications, which France communicated without hesitation to this friend of Prussia, is even more impressive. It included the reduction of Prussia to the boundaries of 1866 and restoration of the dispossessed; enlargement of the middle states at the expense of ancient Prussian territory, and "constitution of state groups in Germany which would permanently break the Prussian supremacy." This formula expresses the well-known aim of dividing Germany into as many equally large states as possible, the aim which had been made the basis of the Franco-Austrian negotiations of 1869. No evidence is necessary to prove that in this grouping the neutralized Rhineland state with a generous allotment of territory was to play an important part and would in a sense have symbolized the federalistic dismemberment of Germany.

In one respect the war aims communicated by Gramont to the Russians contain a surprise—a feature which at the same time explains the reason why they were communicated at all. At the end the French minister asked the Russian government the official question what it planned to do if the French army should reach Berlin and offer Danzig to Russia in return for her neutrality. This free disposition of German territory, which thus revealed designs even against the eastern German frontier, is the last official expression of the French war aims, made only a short time before the first skirmish at Weissenburg.

In the light of all these French plans, which, be it noted, must be regarded as minimum demands, it becomes clear how perfidious was the war manifesto wherein Napoleon announced to the world his desire that "the peoples forming the great Germanic nation shall be free to control their own destinies." The announcement of the manifesto that it was planned to establish an order "guaranteeing our security for the future" is of the same ilk. The persistent use of such phrases for centuries did not serve to make them more plausible. The picture of the Germany of the Peace of Westphalia, exposed on every side to invasion and disruption, and with all internal bonds loosened to a degree of utter defenselessness—this was the historical ideal of the past which dominated the plans of the present. It was "the great idea" of the French policy, according to Thiers, to disorganize the German state to such an extent that security and aggrandizement would fall to the happy lot of its French neighbor.

Against this menace, which had barely been avoided in 1866, the Germans had to defend their unity and independence in 1870. In this latter year it was the last echo of those Napoleonic speculations which we discovered as being the secret forces impelling the empire for the seven years between 1863 and 1870. But during a more recent period of seven years, from 1919 to 1926, we have learned by experience that the rhythm of French history is still guided by its initial principle, that this nation, impelled by the force of tradition, can not resist the evil temptations which surround it.

The policy of Napoleon and the French, which opposed Germany's national right of self-determination, led to the war of 1870. Was it justifiable for this policy to defend its fateful course of action before the bars of history by pleading the "security" of France? Is such justification admissible? We have seen how after 1866 the motive of security gradually met the requirements of the new situation and supplanted that of aggrandizement. But it was only a new name for an old concept—the concept of national frontiers, Romano-Gallic reminiscences, pseudo-historical feudal rights and other attempts to clothe gross reality in a palliating mantle of ideas. Two generations earlier the attainment of the national frontiers had been looked upon in France as a sacred tradition. "It is the doctrine of the scholar," said Sorel, "the creed of the poet, the ambition of the popular leader, of the kings, the ministers, the generals, the political meetings, and the committees; it is a question of interests for the economist, a reason of state for the politician, a national dream." All these spheres of life forthwith seized upon the motive of security, and thus revived once more a great historical tradition. This tradition, though it spoke in terms of defense, had in reality an offensive purpose, for it strove to disturb or diminish the national unity of its neighbor. It was animated by the theory that its own security, unity and peace could be maintained only if that neighbor were doomed to insecurity, disunity and unrest, and in advocating this theory it violated the unwritten law of morality which guides the life of nations and sets bounds to the egoism of national interests. The struggles of the past are of interest for the historical consciousness of the European nations only when their motives and impulses live on in the present as a determining factor. The line which runs from Louis XIV directly to Napoleon III becomes in the end a prime cause for the war of 1870–1871. This fact was clear to the generation which fought that war. To the numerous judgments of other nations we may add the opinion of the American minister Bancroft, the renowned historian. On October 12, 1870, he spoke the following confidential words in the Berlin foreign office:

> *The leading statesmen as well as public opinion in America regard the present war essentially as an act of self-defence on Germany's part, and the outstanding task is to insure Germany permanently, by a better system of frontiers, against new wars of aggression on the part of her western neighbors, of which the past three centuries have brought so large a number.*

The real facts began to be obscured when, with the formation of the great coalition against Germany, the French conception was adopted by the political allies of France. And since the World War the question of the causes of the war of 1870 was, for political reasons, still more obscured and supplanted by a legend which described the latter as merely a step preliminary to the former. The causes of both wars were merged in one large question of guilt, so presented that those who, in France or in countries intellectually dependent upon her, believed in the exclusive or principal responsibility of Germany for the World War, were led to believe also the legend that France was attacked by Germany in 1870. But while the French undertook to reconstruct a fictitious past and to invent the story of the French lamb and the German wolf, it happened that the newly aroused spirit of their historical Rhineland policy, endowed with a new halo and unhampered by diplomatic considerations, has in recent years since the World War given ever more damaging testimony of them. What we have detected as the secret motive power of French politics ever since 1815 and as the Napoleonic ambition which from 1863 on led to the catastrophe, now became more irresistible than ever before. Almost all parties, with a few exceptions, now endorsed the claim for the Rhine, and all along the line scholarship, animated by a spirit which Albert Sorel had once castigated, argued the historical right of that claim, enlisting self-interest and sentiment in the service of a consistent endeavor, which varied but in the details of method and advocated now annexation pure and simple and now some form of Rhineland state, either neutral or at least independent of Prussia and in any case exposed to penetration. This device, of course, had always been the first step toward conquest, and during the dark days of confusion after 1919 it found, even in Germany, sympathetic fools and treacherous advocates who did not realize whose interests would be served by any change in the estalished order along the Rhine.

If the causes of the war of 1870 are to be linked and associated with those of the World War, well and good. History justifies such a procedure, but not in the sense in which the enemies of Germany, who would make her alone responsible for the World War, interpret it. The French national tradition which drove Napoleon III into the war and brought about the fateful clash between the historical Rhineland policy of the French and the right of self-determination of the German people is the cradle of that spirit of revenge which played so important a part in bringing about the international tension leading to the World War. The same spirit which inspired the secret forces of the French national soul has imposed upon it a large measure of guilt before the bars of mankind. Inasmuch as this spirit prevents a permanent reconciliation of the two nations after the catastrophe, it has remained to this day the most serious obstruction to all hopes for future pacific intercourse among the nations of Europe.

Émile Ollivier
THE ETERNAL BOCHE

The last fifty years of Émile Ollivier's life were one long anticlimax. After winning an early reputation as a brilliant lawyer, he had plunged into the turbulent politics of the Second Empire. His forceful agitation in favor of

From Émile Ollivier, *The Franco-Prussian War and Its Hidden Causes* (Boston: Little, Brown and Company, 1912), pp. 5–9, 400–404.

parliamentary rule led to his appointment as prime minister early in 1870.
It was an unfortunate time to be in power in Paris. Seven months later he
was forced to resign in the midst of defeat during the Franco-Prussian War.
Thereafter there was nothing for him to do but meditate on the glories of
the past and seek vicarious vengeance against Bismarck in his voluminous
memoirs. His death in 1913 came on the eve of another war which was to
reverse the verdict of Sedan.

The first cause of the war of 1870 is to be found in the year 1866. It
was in that year, to be marked forever with black, it was in that year
of blindness when one error was redeemed only by a more grievous
error, and when the infirmities of the government were made mortal
by the bitterness of the opposition; it was in that accursed year that
was born the supreme peril of France and of the empire. If the year
1870 is the terrible year, 1866 is the fatal year. The Romans according
to Cicero, considered the battle of the Allia more disastrous than the
taking of Rome because that last misfortune was the result of the first.

Everybody, in all Europe as well as in France, is in accord touching
the importance of the fateful year, and this historic truth is not contested. But everywhere the error committed by Napoleon III is mistakenly characterized. It was his chimerical loyalty to the principle of
nationalities, people say, which led him to allow Prussia to constitute
a great power that was a menace to ourselves. Say just the contrary,
and you will be in right. It was his disloyalty to the principle of nationalities that was the source of all of Napoleon III's misfortunes
and our own.

People would not deny it if they had a better comprehension of this
theory of nationalities, which everybody talks about without understanding it, or understanding it all awry. The theory of nationalities
may be reduced to a few maxims of luminous simplicity:

> Every freely constituted nation forms a sovereign, intangible organism,
> however weak, which cannot be placed under foreign domination without
> its consent, or be kept there against its will. It does not recognize con-
> quest as a legitimate means of acquisition. Only the will of the people
> has the power lawfully to create, to transform, to diminish, or to increase
> kingdoms.
> Whence it follows: first, that no nation has the right to meddle in the
> affairs of another, to object to its international arrangements, to prevent
> it from separating from a state to which it was united by force, or from
> annexing itself to another to which it is drawn by its sympathies or its

interests. Furthermore, Europe, assembled in congress or conference, is not possessed of a collective right of its own, which is denied to each nation separately, on the pretext of preventing any nation from disturbing, at its pleasure, the general system to which it belongs.

The underlying principle of the theory of nationalities is easily distinguishable from others with which it is too often confused—that of great agglomerations, of natural boundaries, and of race. The will of the people concerned may, if it seems fitting, constitute great agglomerations, but it may constitute small ones as well. It does not recognize natural frontiers. The real frontiers are those established by the will of the people; the others are the walls of a prison, which one has always the right to tear down. Woe to the country that drags a province in its train like a millstone about its neck; woe to that one whose people do not bask in its sunshine with free and joyful hearts. To create moral unity is more essential than to satisfy the strategic demands of a mountain-chain or a stream.

Nor does the theory of nationalities recognize a pretended right of race, manifested by a common language or by historic tradition, by virtue of which all the nations born of a common stock and speaking the same language must needs, whether they will or no, and without being consulted, be united in a single state. The idea of race is a barbarous, exclusive, retrograde idea, and has nothing in common with the broad, sacred, civilizing idea of fatherland. Race has limits which cannot be overstepped; fatherland has none; it may expand and develop unceasingly; it might become all mankind, as under the Roman Empire. On our European continent races long since became blended in fatherlands, and it would be impossible to undo the mysterious process from which have flowed the beautiful products of that blending.

There is an ineffable sweetness in the word fatherland, just because it expresses, not a preordained aggregation, but a free, loving creation, wherein millions of human beings have placed their hearts for centuries past.

The will of the peoples, then, is the one dominant, sovereign, absolute principle, whence the modern law of nations in its entirety should flow by a series of logical deductions, as from an inexhaustible spring. It is the principle of liberty substituted in international relations for geographical and historical inevitableness.

Of course the principle of nationality does not do away with all wars. There remain the wars waged for honor, for religion, for the diversion of despots; but it eliminates the most common and most dangerous sort—those of conquest; and it tends toward the progressive abolition of other wars, by virtue of the civilizing principle which is its inspiration. It should be cultivated everywhere with respect, and propagated by men of progress and liberty. In France it should be a national dogma, since it is our incontestable right to reconquer our dear Alsace, brutally wrested from us by conquest, and annexed to the foreigner without her consent.

Were the events that occurred in Germany in 1866 the logical outcome of the principle of nationalities? Was it by virtue of that principle as we have defined it, that Prussia annexed the Danish Duchies, the free towns, Frankfurt, Hesse-Darmstadt, and Hanover, although it was the declared desire of the peoples thereof to retain their autonomy? No, it was by virtue of a denial of that principle that those annexations were carried out. Bismarck, who was not fond of hypocritical euphemisms of speech, said in so many words, "It was by right of conquest." The year 1866, therefore, was not the triumph of the principle of nationality, but its defeat, and the victorious resurrection of the principle of conquest. The real error of Napoleon III consisted, not in forwarding that civilizing principle, which had already raised him so high, but in becoming the compliant tool, in the hope of a reward, of those who were rending it with their swords.

He was at liberty not to oppose by force the conquest of Prussia, if he did not consider that the interest of France demanded it; but he should have seconded the efforts which others (Russia, for example) were making to arrest them, and, in any event, should not have approved, much less have encouraged them, and, less still, have demanded a reward for that encouragement. But that is what he did: he gave Prussia his formal assent, refused to second Russia in suggesting the assembling of a congress, and solicited, as a reward, first the left bank of the Rhine, then Belgium, and finally Luxembourg.

Prussia welcomed his adhesion with sarcastic cordiality, and refused with insolent ingratitude the wage, even when it was reduced to the minimum. She did more: she snapped her fingers at the man to whose kindly neutrality she was indebted for not being crushed on the battlefield, and she instantly disregarded the promise she had made at Prague to arrest her predominance at the Main: she passed that boundary, in a military sense, by means of treaties of alliance, and thus constituted the military unity of Germany—the only form of unity which was dangerous to us. . . .

The cause of the conflict between Germany and France was only one of those "artificial fatalities," born of the false conceptions or unhealthy ambitions of statesmen, which with lapse of time become worn out, transformed, and often extinguished. If France had but resolutely made up her mind not to meddle in the affairs of Germany, not to regard German unity as a menace or as a lessening of her own importance, it would have seemed perfectly natural to her that a nation so powerful in every way—in intelligence, imagination, poetry, science, and arms—should shape herself as she chose, with full liberty of spontaneous action.

On the other hand, if the German professors, content with the memories of 1814 and of Waterloo, could but have made up their minds to forget the Palatinate and Jena, on the instant this alleged fatality of war would have vanished, and the only relation between the two nations, established by mutual consent, would have been one of friendly cooperation in the common task of spreading light and of emancipation from real fatalities. That was the hope to which I devoted my conduct in international matters, and which, as minister, I would have brought to fruition had my power endured.

But there was a man to whom it was important that that artificial fatality should exist and should end in war. It was that powerful genius, who, not choosing to abandon to time the glory of achieving slowly the work of unity, whose hour of triumph was inevitable, determined to hasten the evolution, to force upon the present what the future would have accomplished freely, and to retain for himself alone the glory which his successors would otherwise have shared. With him out of the way, war between France and Germany would have ceased to be predestined, and the son of Napoleon III would have escaped it as well as his father.

Napoleon III wanted peace, but with a vacillating will; Bismarck wanted war, with an inflexible will: the inflexible will overcame the vacillating will. A fresh proof, as that profound thinker Gustave Le Bon so forcibly says, that "the faith that raises mountains is named the will. It is the true creator of things."

So that it is a pitiful thing to read these labored dissertations of our trumpery historians, searching for what they call responsibilities, and struggling to incriminate, some the statesmen of the opposition, others those of the government. Unquestionably the opposition were so short-sighted as to keep alive an irritable agitation in men's minds; unquestionably the emperor should not have reopened, by a fruitless demand of guaranties, a question already closed by a triumphant solution. But neither the declamations of the opposition, nor the mistake of Napoleon III, were the decisive cause of the war. No Frenchman was responsible for it. The only man who will have the glory or the shame of it, whichever posterity may adjudge it to be, is the man of iron, whose indomitable and heroic will controlled events and made them serve his ambition.

Demosthenes said to the Athenians: "Let an orator rise and say to you: 'It is Diopithus who causes all your ills; it is Chares, or Aristophon,' or any other that it pleases him to name, and instantly you applaud and exclaim loudly, 'Oh! how truly he speaks!' But let a plain-spoken man say to you: 'O Athenians! the sole author of your ills is Philip'—that truth angers you; it is even as an arrow that wounds you." And I say to our Athenians: "The war was let loose upon us neither by Diopithus, nor by Chares, nor by Aristophon, but by Philip, and in 1870 Philip's name was Bismarck."

One of Bismarck's panegyrists, Johannes Scherr, has described most excellently the character that should be attributed to the creator of German unity.

After producing so many giants of thought, Germany was destined to produce, at last, a hero of deeds. In the age of the Reformation, and later, we had had an abundance of idealists, but not a politician. We lacked the practical genius, the genius unhampered by schedules. Yes, just that, in very truth! For reflecting and experienced men must needs leave where it deserves to be, that is to say, in the child's primer, the worn-out commonplace which declares that "the most honest politician is the best." There has never been such a thing as an honest politician, in the ordinary sense of the phrase, and there ought never to be. The creative statesman should perform his allotted task without taking pains to find out whether his adversaries consider it "dishonest," or whether it is unpleasant or harmful to them. It is not the ethereal arguments of a subjective idealism, but stern realities, super-prosaic material interests, as well as commonplace and exalted passions, which in combination make the science of statecraft.

Thus would Bismarck have liked to be praised—in such terms it is fitting to speak of that extraordinary man, the craftiest of foxes, the boldest of lions, who had the art of fascinating and of terrifying, of making of truth itself an instrument of falsehood; to whom gratitude, forgiveness of injuries, and respect for the vanquished were as entirely unknown as all other noble sentiments save that of devotion to his country's ambition; who deemed legitimate everything that contributes to success and who, by his contempt for the importunities of morality, dazzled the imagination of mankind.

After the affair of the Duchies, as our ambassador, Talleyrand, was seeking some roundabout phrase by which to express a certain degree of disapproval, "Don't put yourself out," said Bismarck, "nobody but my King thinks that I acted honorably."

Aesthetically, I like him thus. So long as he denies the evidence, plays the virtuous, the guileless man, outdoes himself in tartufferie, he lowers himself to the point of making himself contemptible. As soon as he reveals his true self and boasts of his audacious knaveries which raised his Germany, until then divided and impotent, to the first rank among the nations, then he is as great as Satan—a Satan beautiful to look upon. Bismarck hatching in the dark the Hohenzollern candidacy, without a suspicion that war will inevitably be the result, would be a zany to be hooted at; Bismarck devising that same plot because it is the sole means of causing the outbreak of the war which he must have in order to achieve the unity of his fatherland, is a mighty statesman, of sinister but impressive grandeur. He will not thereby have opened for himself the gates of any Paradise; he will have won forever one of the most exalted places in the German Pantheon of terrestrial apotheoses.

Hans Rothfels
A HISTORIC NECESSITY

No one has defended Bismarck with greater perception and understanding than Hans Rothfels. A lifelong opponent of totalitarianism in all its varieties, he left Germany for America during the Third Reich. But for him there is a world of difference between the ideals of the Iron Chancellor and those of National Socialism. As for the unification of Germany, there was no alternative to the policy of blood and iron. Bismarckian diplomacy admittedly relied on power, but it was power used with moderation and restraint. In his article on "Problems of a Bismarck Biography" Rothfels takes issue with Erich Eyck's interpretation of the founder of the German Empire.

This brings the discussion back to Mr. Eyck's underlying assumption that the German national unity which he himself finds natural, would have been attainable by other and less forceful means than those of Bismarck. This is a hypothesis which, of course, can neither be proved nor repudiated. It can be said, however, and in view of many legends it seems a matter of fairness to do so today, that there was little "western" sympathy with the attempt at founding a "good" German Reich, that is, one on the liberal-democratic basis of 1848. While Disraeli spoke of "the 50 mad professors at Frankfurt," Palmerston felt alarmed by the development of a *"nation inconnue jusqu'ici au Foreign Office."* And Thiers later confessed that if he could have had his way in 1848 he would have extended the French frontiers to the Rhine and taken "the keys of Germany" into hand. When it eventually came to the half-liberal policy of union in 1850 it ended with a deadlock enforced by a Russo-Austrian ultimatum. Even Radowitz's very moderate aims would have to be carried out by arms. Nor was the diplomatic record of the new era in Prussia altogether promising. When the liberal policy of moral conquest was at its height in 1860, the *London Times* had this to say:

> *Prussia is always leaning on somebody, always getting somebody to help her, never willing to help herself; always ready to deliberate, never to decide; present in congresses, but absent in battles; speaking and writing, never for or against, but only on, the question; ready to supply any*

Reprinted by permission of the publisher, from Hans Rothfels, "Problems of a Bismarck Biography," *Review of Politics* 4 (1947): 375–380.

amount of ideals or sentiments, but shy of anything that savors of the real or the actual. She has a large army, but notoriously one in no condition for fighting. She is profuse in circulars and notes, but has generally a little to say for both sides. No one counts on her as a friend, no one dreads her as an enemy. How she became a Great Power history tells us, why she remains so nobody can tell. . . . Prussia unaided could not keep the Rhine or the Vistula for a month from her ambitious neighbors.

Mr. Eyck has a rather optimistic view of these ambitious neighbors, in particular of the French tradition of advancing to the east, a view which was shared neither by the German socialists circa 1860 nor by the lauded Konstantin Frantz for that matter. It seems worthy of mentioning that the federalist thinker started from the very assumption of a double threat to *Mitteleuropa*. He therefore advocated a universal system in the center of the continent with a voluntary union of the historic states as its nucleus, a loose German and non-German federation, which Holland, Sweden, Denmark might join and England might protect. Such a system would guarantee peace by turning Russia's and France's ambitions to Asia and North Africa repectively. One may pay high tribute to this idealistic scheme and yet seriously doubt its chance of overcoming particularism by persuasion or achieving a British willingness to enter upon Central European commitments and to sympathize with the economic perspectives of a great federative bloc (united by mutual preferences!). It is only in an entirely different situation, against the background of a post-Bismarckian development and with foreign powers ruling over Central Europe, that the federalist concept or rather that of a "Central European Switzerland" has gained a new meaning.

It would appear then that the consolidation of the weak center of Europe presupposed other means than those suggested by Frantz and that the nucleus had to be created by diplomatic action rather than by a plea for sympathy or a moral appeal. Whether war was absolutely necessary may be doubted and certainly can not be demonstrated. But it is definitely wrong to say that only the forceful foundation of the Reich of 1871 produced the *cauchemar des coalitions* as a sort of self-inflicted punishment. The conviction of a double threat was not of Bismarck's making. It had been widespread among the liberals of Germany around 1860 in the same sense as it was shared by Frantz. And it was the basis of Bismarck's diplomacy be-

fore 1870 just as much as afterwards it was simply a Central European fact. Only by a new distribution of power and a new security, in
Bismarck's view, could the aim be reached (which he had in common
with Frantz), of turning Russia's and France's ambitions "to Asia
and North Africa respectively."

This criticism of some federalist illusions, however, should not
prevent us from seeing that the pre- or supra-national and anti-cen-
tralistic elements in the structure of Bismarck's Reich came nearer
to a basic federalism than is ordinarily realized. On this point Mr.
Eyck's book falls particularly short of the mark. The fact that Bismarck stressed the institutional links between the old German
Confederation and the new Reich, that he checked the Reichstag
and its universal suffrage by the "anonymous-phalanx" of the federative council, that he kept the competence of the central organs within
very narrow limits, that he resisted successfully a responsible
Reichsministry—all this was, in the author's view, mere tactics and
only meant to concentrate the real power in Prussia and, in the last
analysis, in Bismarck's hands. There is truth in this interpretation,
not a new one for that matter, but it is by far not the full truth or
the most substantial part of it. Again all evidences are omitted which
refer to some of the underlying principles. It is certainly not uninter-
esting and beside the point to recall today such principles as Bismarck expressed in the Reichstag (April 16, 1869): ". . . In Germanic
states one should not ask . . . what can be in common, how far can
the great mouth of the commonwealth swallow the apple (*hinein-
beissen in den Apfel*)—but rather one should ask: what must be
absolutely in common." It seems safe to say that Bismarck, quite
apart from other elements of his thought, was Junker enough to be
antitotalitarian in principle. More consideration should also be given
to his plans to supplement the Reichstag by *staendische* organizations. Particularly in connection with the plan for compulsory insurance against accidents, he thought of a network of professional
associations to be spread over the country. This again implies antiparliamentary tactics but also an insight into the dangerous process
of social atomization. While in all this there was a federalist aspect
domestically, the noncentralistic setup of the Reich had a broader
meaning as a pattern of transition to other federative forms beyond
the frontiers: Germany with her composite character might indicate,

as Bismarck pointed out, a method by the use of which "Austria could reach a reconciliation of the political and material interests which exist between the eastern frontiers of the Russians and the Bay of Cattaro."

These potentialities are often overlooked. They are certainly not seen by Mr. Eyck and he seems to be completely and rather naively unaware of the nationalist implications of a unitary and democratic German Reich in Central Europe or of Bruck's "Greater Germany." In contrast Bismarck's national state was no "nation state" proper; it included non-Germans (about 10 percent) and it did not include and ought not to have included all Germans. Jokingly Bismarck once said that, if the nine million contiguous Germans in Austria ever would try to join the Reich, he would wage war against them. In more serious words he admonished them, that instead of harking back, they should take the lead in evolving a multi-national combine in the southeast. The same restraint he observed towards the Germans in Russia, and he did so not only for diplomatic or opportunistic reasons. His so-called *étatisme* may have been a major limitation in some aspects of domestic policy; but what was opposition to democracy was at the same time opposition to nationalism. What was an attempt at checking social atomism was paralleled by a check on the trend towards a national atomism which would disintegrate Central Europe and end in a war of races. That is why Bismarck opposed Pan-Germanism no less than Pan-Slavism.

In this negative attitude—or rather in this conservative restraint— there was implied some positive appraisal of variety and multi-national forms of life. There was at least much more of it than liberal and federalist critics usually realize. The crown prince may have been thunderstruck when Bismarck, in 1870, admonished him to have his son learn the Polish language or when he added that all the Prussian rulers down to Frederick the Great had known it—and that he knew it himself. To the liberal biographer these remarks do not seem to have made any more sense than they probably made to the crown prince. Incidentally, Mr. Eyck does not speak of the anti-Polish settlement law of 1886 (*Ansiedlungsgesetz*) which ranks so high on the list of Prussian *hakatism*. As a matter of fact the settlement of German peasants in the eastern provinces was urged by the national liberals. Bismarck yielded to them but professed no sympathy with uprooting the Polish peasants or depriving them of their language. In his old age he spoke of the intermingling of peoples in the east as "riches willed by God." Whatever the shortcomings of this Polish policy he was certainly as remote from racialism and biologism as anyone could be. . . .

But the writer does not want this article to end on a note of professional controversy. There is more at stake than that. We may criticize Bismarck for many good reasons, for paving the way to some fatal trends of our days, but while doing so we cannot very well overlook the fundamental fact that Hitler, in almost every respect, did precisely what the founder of the Reich had refused to do. Many of those who were under the heel or outside Germany, had an appreciation of this fact. And thus the word of the Danish historian may be taken up once more as a summary which draws the essential frontier line: Bismarck certainly "belonged to our world," that is, to the anti-Hitlerian world. That this was not generally realized is in part the fault of Germans and German historians themselves. But it may be called a kind of saving grace that a revival of genuine Bismarckian thought (as different from the old Bismarck orthodoxy) was one of the forces which went into the making of the German resistance against Hitler. Specifically "Prussian" elements as far as they remained alive after the landslide of 1933 were also in the anti-Nazi camp. To state this is no longer a matter of any practical importance since these forces have been radically eliminated, but it seems to be a matter of historical justice.

IV ARBITER OF EUROPE

Erich Brandenburg

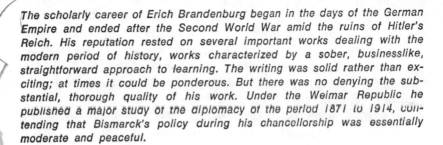

PAX TEUTONICA

The scholarly career of Erich Brandenburg began in the days of the German Empire and ended after the Second World War amid the ruins of Hitler's Reich. His reputation rested on several important works dealing with the modern period of history, works characterized by a sober, businesslike, straightforward approach to learning. The writing was solid rather than exciting; at times it could be ponderous. But there was no denying the substantial, thorough quality of his work. Under the Weimar Republic he published a major study of the diplomacy of the period 1871 to 1914, contending that Bismarck's policy during his chancellorship was essentially moderate and peaceful.

The supreme object of Germany's policy, which was controlled by Bismarck until 1890 in spite of various *contretemps,* was the maintenance of European peace. It was not merely stressed in the speeches and manifestoes of our leading men; it was the governing motive in the whole disposition of our policy and in the particular decisions which had to be taken. Knowledge of this has become the common property of historians since the German archives bearing on the Bismarck period have been thrown open for research, no matter what views may be held as to the great chancellor's political conduct or even as to his intentions in particular instances. Our great statesman was of the opinion that we had everything we really needed and that war, even a victorious war, did not offer an actual gain. On the north and the west our territory had actually reached and occasionally even exceeded the limits of our nationality. No thoughtful German has ever wanted to add German Switzerland or Holland to our empire. To bring the German provinces of Austria once more into our national state has seemed to many a desirable aim, and to not a few simply a matter of duty. Nevertheless it was in Catholic southern Germany that these aspirations flourished rather than in the Protestant north which had taken the leading part in the new empire. Bismarck always maintained that the inclusion of the Catholic German Austrians would strengthen the centrifugal

From Erich Brandenburg, *From Bismarck to the World War: A History of German Foreign Policy, 1870–1914* (London, 1927), pp. 2–5, 8–10. Reprinted by permission of the Oxford University Press.

forces within the empire; but on the other hand he considered the collapse of Austria a national danger, as the majority of the non-German territories were inhabited by a Slav population who would naturally turn to Russia if the Hapsburg monarchy were dissolved. Such an accession to Russia's power seemed to him ominous both for Germany and for Europe. Hence the maintenance of Austria-Hungary's position as a Great Power became one of the corner-stones of his policy; and so long as he was at the helm and his influence persisted, all thoughts of increase of territory in the south-east were barred. As a matter of fact in the northeast we had already more foreign elements in our empire than was comfortable. To increase the percentage of Polish inhabitants hostile to us would have been a huge blunder. Bismarck never believed that the Baltic provinces, the ruling classes in which were German both by descent and culture, could ever again be drawn into our empire. Geograph-ically these provinces lay too much outside our territory. The ma-jority of their inhabitants were of a different race and were not friendly to us, while even the nobility were much too sympathetic towards Russia—where they played a big part and received special consideration—to wish for union with Germany.

These facts and considerations led Bismarck to the conclusion that we had nothing to gain even from a victorious war in Europe. Besides, our newly-created empire was, so to speak, still in process of formation; time alone would test the new arrangements and prove their worth; sharp differences in religious and social matters consti-tuted a serious menace to us; and, finally, our budding prosperity urgently required peace. Maintenance of existing conditions and of peace had to be the cardinal point of German policy. Bismarck recognized this and acted upon it. In his *Thoughts and Recollections* he declares that his aim was to earn the confidence of lesser and greater powers by a peaceful, just, honest and conciliatory policy. It almost sounds like a belated palliation of his essentially Machia-vellian statesmanship. Yet the further we carry our researches, the clearer is the evidence that he was only putting into words the fundamental principle of his actions.

Such being the general position of affairs at that time, what was there to disturb the peace of Europe? There were two centers of constant unrest, two territories whose temporary status was not generally recognized as the foundation of future troubles—Alsace-Lorraine and the Balkans.

At the Peace of Frankfurt, France had been compelled to renounce Alsace-Lorraine. It had been a bitter mortification to her to part with land that for well-nigh two centuries had formed an integral part of her national territory. She overlooked the fact that she had previously conquered by force these provinces from Germany. The demand for their restoration was regarded as an injustice to France and to the territory itself, whose inhabitants were not consulted. Thenceforward the great majority of the French nation regarded it as a matter of course that by some means or other this injustice should be redressed. The loss of the Saar territory in the second Treaty of Paris in 1815 had not been forgotten. Even in 1866, Napoleon III had made an attempt to recover it. Of course the explanation of the French attitude towards Germany's injustice was to be found not only in the loss of territory, but also in the supersession of her dominating position in Europe: after the Prussian victories of 1866 the cry for revenge made itself heard. Anger at military defeat accentuated it. The emergence of a new military German Empire, economically superior, betokened the end of the French hegemony and wounded French pride in its most sensitive spot. Alsace-Lorraine was the outward and visible symbol of the overthrow France had suffered.

French statesmen thoroughly understood that nothing could be done in the immediate future towards realizing these hopes of revenge. France's wounds must be healed, her internal affairs reorganized, her military strength brought up to a far different standard, before she could think of a new war. Well they knew that even later on a struggle of that kind could scarcely be waged single-handed with any prospect of success. Germany was steadily increasing in population and industrial wealth. The population of France was not increasing, her ancient wealth was virtually stationary, while in actual industrial enterprise there was no comparison with Germany. Hence the need of finding allies, and of exploiting every development in the general political situation unfavorable to Germany. France's leading men were firmly convinced that her hour would come when Germany became involved in a war with a third power. German policy had therefore to reckon that in any serious conflict with another power, France would be against her. Therein lay the significance of the Alsace-Lorraine problem in European politics. It was not in itself an acute danger, but it was a latent and persistent threat to peace, because it was evident that in every conceivable situation it would determine France's attitude and would be an unseen factor influencing the grouping of the powers. There were certainly men and tendencies in France who loyally accepted the conditions of the Peace of Frankfurt, who sought to repair their losses in other ways and wished to live at peace with Germany. Occasionally they were even countenanced officially. But they were always an object of suspicion to the Nationalists, regarded by them as traitors in disguise to the most sacred feelings of the French nation, and at decisive moments they could be thrust aside by an easily-roused popular agitation. . . .

As Bismarck's policy aimed at the maintenance of peace, it was of urgent importance for him to prevent any political disturbance of the peace either by the latent problem of Alsace-Lorraine, or by the open problem in the Near East. Hence two of the leading features of his policy must be to isolate France as much as possible so as to make a war of revenge out of the question, and to induce Russia and Austria to come to a settlement in the Near East, or at least to prevent them from coming to an open breach.

In order to isolate France it was advisable for Germany to get into touch as closely as possible with those states upon whose alliance France might count in the event of a war of revenge, among them Russia, Italy, and Austria. Even after 1871 there was a strong desire on the part of Austria to regain the position she had lost in 1866 should a favorable opportunity occur. A revival of the old coalition of the days of Frederick the Great—France, Austria and Russia—which Bismarck had long dreaded, was by no means so improbable as it seemed to a later generation. The League of the Three Emperors in the seventies, later on the Austro-German Triple Alliance, and the various treaties of security with Russia, all served a common end. An understanding with England was more than once considered, particularly during the Eastern crisis of 1875–1879, but all efforts failed because Bismarck stipulated for unconditional guarantees for the occupation of Alsace-Lorraine, and to this English statesmen would not consent. Even when they came into sharp conflict with France in 1882 over the occupation of Egypt, they were not to be won over. Towards the close of the eighties, when France and Russia began to draw together, Bismarck again proposed in London an alliance with England, sanctioned by Parliament, for mutual defense against an attack by France. He laid stress at that time on the fact that the knowledge that such a treaty existed would of itself be instrumental in preventing war. Lord Salisbury, who was then foreign secretary, was inclined to favor this suggestion. But some months later, when Count Herbert Bismarck was sent to London by his father to negotiate the Samoan question, and took the opportunity of mentioning the possibility of an alliance, Lord Salisbury held distinctly aloof. He reminded him of the parliamentary control of English policy and of the influence of public opinion which would not be easily won over to an alliance.

In spite of these efforts to isolate France, Bismarck's policy towards the latter was in no sense hostile. He wished to prevent France from disturbing the peace and from undoing the terms of the Treaty of Frankfurt, and he endeavored to establish as friendly relations as possible between Berlin and Paris. He went so far as to assure France of Germany's active support in all questions where their mutual interests did not conflict and to consent to her conquest of Annam and Tonquin. He encouraged France in her occupation of Tunis and repeatedly drew her attention to Morocco as a suitable field for her colonial activity. He hoped that a successful colonial policy would in some measure satisfy the French love of prestige, and that the new colonial empire would in time provide compensation for Alsace-Lorraine, so that possibly in the course of a few decades the thought of revenge might die out. He himself well knew that this was but a slender hope. Nevertheless he intended to leave nothing undone that could tranquillize and conciliate.

R. W. Seton-Watson

À TROIS IN A WORLD GOVERNED BY FIVE

Robert William Seton-Watson won an international reputation as an authority on Eastern Europe. He was throughout his life sympathetic to the cause of the Slavic peoples, and during the First World War helped win for them the right of national self-determination. In the 1930s, moreover, he published what is probably still the best one-volume account of British foreign policy during the nineteenth century. While the focus of the work is the diplomacy pursued by Downing Street, the author pays tribute to the astute statesmanship of Bismarck, emphasizing particularly its effect on the position of England in the Mediterranean.

It is hardly necessary to point out that the eclipse of France in 1870 completely altered the distribution of forces in Europe, and ushered in the period of "Armed Peace." The achievement of German unity under the auspices of Prussia, sealed by the annexation of Alsace-Lorraine, left Germany predominant on the Continent; France, exhausted by her defeats and by sanguinary civil dissensions, found herself completely isolated abroad, and the legend of her decadence was widely disseminated and believed. In Austria-Hungary the French defeats determined the failure of the federalist experiment, and the fall of the Francophil Beust, who was succeeded as Foreign Minister by Count Julius Andrássy, meant not merely the triumph of the Dual System and a virtual Hungarian predominance inside that system, but in foreign policy the beginnings of a rapprochement with Germany which was eventually to develop into the Triple Alliance. Meanwhile Spain had long since ceased to be a great power, while Italy was still consolidating her new position. Thus Britain's attitude in the war of 1870 had resulted both in her own isolation and in the temporary eclipse of the Western and Liberal powers as a serious factor in the European balance. But parallel with this there was a revival, in the years following the war, of the old alliance of the three Eastern Courts—the Three Emperors' League, as it was now called

From R. W. Seton-Watson, *Britain in Europe, 1789–1914: A Survey of Foreign Policy* (New York, 1937), pp. 501–502, 549–550, 563–565. Reprinted by permission of the Cambridge University Press.

—a combination wellnigh irresistible so long as it held together. In its essence, it stood for the same ideals of conservatism and authoritative government as the earlier Holy Alliance—toned down, it is true, in Germany and Austria-Hungary to meet the requirements of the time, but none the less effectually resting upon dynastic control of military and foreign affairs—opposed to popular control wherever possible, and united by a further bond in the common necessity of preventing the resurrection of Poland. . . .

Without entering upon an analysis of the Bismarckian policy, it is possible to reduce its essentials to three fundamental axioms—at all costs to prevent a Franco-Russian alliance such as might force Germany to fight on two fronts, and at all costs to avert any situation in which it might be necessary for Germany to choose between Russia and Austria-Hungary, since a contest between these two powers might result in a war *à outrance* and in such a dislocation of forces in Eastern Europe as would be excessively dangerous to Germany. General dynastic and conservative principles, as well as common interests in the Polish question, increased still further his desire for a triple accord. "All politics," he told Shuvalov, "reduce themselves to this formula: Try to be *à trois* in a world governed by five powers. I have made an *entente à deux,* in order to return thereafter to an *entente à trois* if you really wish it. . . ."

The astute Bismarck was fully aware of Salisbury's dilemma, and spared no pains to draw Britain into the orbit of the Central Powers, thereby killing two birds with one stone, since he was raising the value of a renewal of the Triple Alliance in the eyes of both Vienna and Rome. Already on 12 February [1887] a secret convention was concluded between Britain and Italy, by which the two powers undertook to uphold the *status quo* in the Mediterranean, Adriatic, Aegean and Black Seas, while Italy accepted the British position in Egypt and Britain bound herself to the support of Italy in the event of "encroachments" in North Africa by another power which, though not named, could only be France. In signing such a document the British government gave to Italy

> *the widest guarantee which any parliamentary state could give, namely, that in the event of a Franco-German war England would actively join that group of states which forms the peace police in the East. No English government can give an absolute guarantee for military or naval co-*

*operation in a future conflict, simply because it is not certain whether
Parliament will fulfill those promises. But so far as Lord Salisbury can
judge he is convinced that England, jointly with Austria and Italy, will
make front against Russia, if Turkey and especially Constantinople should
be threatened. He thinks he can assume the same, but less certainly, if
Austria is attacked by Russia, without touching Turkey. In this case it
would be hard for England to give effective support.*

This document should finally dispel the legend of Salisbury's belief
in isolation, and it is confirmed by his private correspondence with
the queen, from which it transpires that he had made it quite clear
to Count Corti that "England never promised material assistance in
view of an uncertain war, of which the object and cause were unknown," and again, that there never could be any question of Britain
taking part in an aggressive war against France.

Austria-Hungary speedily announced her adherence to the Mediterranean Agreement, and later in the year it was rendered still more
precise by a triangular agreement between London, Vienna and
Rome, for the maintenance of the *status quo* in the Near East, and
for joint action to prevent any cession of territory by Turkey, even
to the point of provisional occupation of Turkish territory. Meanwhile
Spain had entered into a special agreement with Italy to maintain
the Mediterranean *status quo,* and not to lend herself to any action
aimed against Italy, Germany and Austria-Hungary.

At this stage Bismarck, who from the background had never
ceased to encourage the three Mediterranean participants, addressed himself directly to Salisbury, and after laying great stress
upon the defensive character of German armed power and on the
impossibility of any change upon the Imperial throne deflecting the
fundamental lines of German policy, reached the conclusion that
France and Russia were the two unstable elements in Europe, and
that Germany would always be obliged to take action, "either if the
independence of Austria-Hungary were threatened by Russian aggression, or if England or Italy were in danger of being set upon by
French armies." Salisbury in his reply went boldly to the root of the
matter by considering the contingency of a Franco-German war. In
that event he credited Russia with a seizure of the straits, a step
from which Britain and Italy alone "would not be sufficient to deter
her," and "all would depend, therefore, on the attitude of Austria,"

who without German help could hardly risk war with Russia. His closing phrase ran,

> *The grouping of states which has been the work of the last year will be an effective barrier against any possible aggression of Russia, and the construction of it will not be among the least services which Your Highness has rendered to the cause of European peace.*

Salisbury was clearly reassured by this correspondence, following as it did upon Bismarck's revelation of the secret clause of the first Austro-German Treaty of 1879; for he had drawn from it the conclusion that "Germany *must* take the side of Austria in any war between Austria and Russia." Needless to say, however, he—and with him all the world, including the government of Vienna—was kept in ignorance of the secret "Reinsurance Treaty" which Bismarck on 18 June 1887 had signed with Russia. Bismarck, it is true, never admitted the charge of perfidy afterwards levelled against him, and definitely wished that the tsar should reveal the treaty to Francis Joseph. But it remains the crowning example of Bismarck's uncanny skill in juggling with four or five conflicting forces, and could not permanently have been kept up by any successor of lesser caliber. It would at any rate seem probable that Bismarck had finally disabused himself of his former suspicions towards Salisbury, whom he had described to St. Vallier at the Congress of Berlin as "ce clergyman laïque obstiné et maladroit."

It is thoroughly characteristic of Bismarck that no sooner had he secured the renewal of the Triple Alliance and reinforced it by the Mediterranean Agreements, than he once more proceeded to woo Russia, as he had done after concluding the Austrian Alliance in 1879. As ever, the key to his policy was his "permanent dread" of an Austro-Russian war, in which he would have to choose between his two allies and to risk the actual collapse of one of them. In the words of Dr. Gooch, "from the crisis which broke up the Dreikaiserbund and brought Austria and Russia to the brink of war, the chancellor's genius extracted securities for the empire he had founded, purchasing the assurance of Russian neutrality in a war provoked by France, by a promise of German neutrality in a war provoked by Austria." The long-drawn Bulgarian crisis enabled him to court Russia more openly than ever before. While all Bulgaria rallied behind the regents in their resistance to Russian dictation, and after no less than eighteen unsuccessful offers of the crown at last secured the acceptance of Prince Ferdinand of Coburg (a young cousin of Queen Victoria and a grandson of Louis Philippe), Bismarck pressed his Russophil orientation to the length of imposing a veto on the marriage of ex-Prince Alexander with the German crown prince and princess's favorite daughter Victoria, lest this should trouble Russo-German relations. In his Reichstag speech of 11 January 1887 he quoted, " 'What's Hecuba to him?' What's Bulgaria to us?" The friendship of Russia was of far greater value, and above all else peace must be kept between Russia and Austria-Hungary. A year later, in the same place (6 February 1888), he balanced his absolute trust in the Tsar's word against the danger of coalitions, and declared, "Think of Austria off the map, and we are isolated, with Italy, between Russia and France. We cannot think Austria away." It was on this occasion that he closed with the memorable words, "We Germans fear God and nothing else in the world." To Frederick III on his deathbed he insisted that the "focussing point" of German policy lay in Russia and in preserving the personal friendship of Alexander III.

Luigi Albertini

JUGGLING ON HORSEBACK
WITH FIVE BALLS

There are few men who can combine an important role in public affairs with significant accomplishment in the world of scholarship. Luigi Albertini was one of them. He first won recognition as a leading Italian journalist in the opening years of the twentieth century. He then entered politics and helped bring Italy into the First World War on the side of the Entente Powers. Under Mussolini he was forced to retire from public life because of his opposition to Fascism, and it was then that he wrote his vast study of the Origins of the War of 1914. The following selection from that work appraises Bismarck's diplomacy in 1887.

From Luigi Albertini, *The Origins of the War of 1914*, 3 vols. (London, 1952–1957), I: 58–62. Reprinted by permission of the Oxford University Press.

Bismarck's precautions were not confined to the renewal of the Triple Alliance. On the day of its signature a Russian semi-official journal, published in Brussels, said that Russia could not pledge herself to neutrality in a new Franco-German war and must hence avoid conflict with Britain and Austria over Eastern questions. This is the thesis which Katkov had for months been propounding in opposition to the views of the Russian Foreign Minister Giers who would have liked to renew the *Dreikaiserbund,* due to lapse in June 1887; but the Tsar opposed this and inclined towards a treaty with Germany alone, a draft for which, drawn up by Giers, was brought to Berlin by Shuvalov. These negotiations presented many difficulties, though they were desired by Bismarck, who was now convinced of the impossibility of getting Vienna and St. Petersburg to accept the division of the Balkans into spheres of influence.

Knowing that the word "aggression" applied to Franco-German relations had an elastic meaning, he would have been content if Russia would give an undertaking to remain neutral in any Franco-German war, but he could not make an equivalent concession in an Austro-Russian war on account of his obligations to Austria-Hungary under the treaty of 1879 which he gave Shuvalov to read. After long discussions the chancellor and the ambassador agreed on a formula binding the two parties to benevolent neutrality in a war of one of them against a third power except in the case that one of the contracting parties directly attacked Austria or France. Germany recognized Russia's historic rights in the Balkans and "the legitimacy of her preponderating and decisive influence in Bulgaria and Eastern Rumelia." The two courts undertook not to permit changes in the *status quo* without previous accord and to oppose any attempted change on which they were not agreed. As regards the Straits, the conditions of the *Dreikaiserbund* remained in force. In an additional protocol Germany undertook to support Russia in reestablishing a regular and legal government in Bulgaria and in opposing the restoration of the Prince of Battenberg.

It was further agreed:

> *If H.M. the Emperor of Russia finds himself compelled to defend the entrance to the Black Sea in order to safeguard his interests, Germany undertakes to observe benevolent neutrality and to give moral and diplo-*

*matic support to such measures as H.M. may deem necessary for the
safety of the key of his Empire.*

This meant that Germany agreed to Russia's taking possession of
the Straits and Constantinople.

This so-called Reinsurance Treaty, made known in 1896, has
roused much discussion and has been described as a breach of
faith. Such was not the view of Bismarck who—as Langer writes—
would have preferred an open agreement if the Tsar, fearing the
effect it might have in Russia, had not insisted on secrecy. The
chancellor who on various occasions had publicly declared that
Germany had no intention of being dragged into a war over the
Balkans and had criticized Austrian policy in the Near East, regarded
the pledges made to Austria as compatible with those he was now
giving to Russia inasmuch as they did not hold good towards whichever of the two powers became an aggressor against the other.
This was the case on the surface, but at bottom in an Austro-
Russian conflict it would have fallen to Bismarck to decide which
party was guilty of the aggression and the interests of Germany
would have obliged him to make this decision accord with German
advantage.

His supreme aim was to prevent the formation of a Franco-
Russian alliance. In France in May 1887 Boulanger was no longer
war minister, and on 1 August Katkov died. However, the Boulangist
movement was still alive in France and found echoes in Russia
where Francophil agitation had friends in the highest circles sur-
rounding the Tsar. To conciliate the latter Bismarck was obliged
to support Russian rather than Austrian demands, as, for instance,
when on 7 July the Bulgarian Assembly offered the throne to Prince
Ferdinand of Saxe-Coburg whom the Russians opposed as an
Austrian tool. The chancellor, acting on the principle of the two
spheres of influence in the Balkans, took the part of Russia and
advised Austria not to move even if Russia took military action in
Bulgaria, a counsel that Austria was not inclined to follow. St.
Petersburg expected him to take active steps to find a solution
favorable to Russia. But this was asking too much and made him
seek to strengthen the Mediterranean coalition of Italy, Austria, and
Britain, extending it in the Austrian interest to the Balkans and

eastern Mediterranean as a counterpoise to Russia, while saving Germany from the odium and risk of thwarting her. Not that Bismarck minded Russian expansion in the Near East. All he sought was to safeguard Austrian interests for which Germany was unwilling to fight. From 7 August 1887 the Italian prime minister and foreign minister (Depretis having died on 29 July) was Francesco Crispi who was determined to break with what he regarded as the pusillanimous policy followed by Italy at the Congress of Berlin and in 1882 when Mancini had declined Granville's invitation to take part in the English expedition into Egypt. Crispi's view was that a more fruitful policy would be to draw closer to the Central Powers and to Britain. On 8 August he expressed his readiness to recognize the election of Prince Ferdinand and went so far as to propose to Salisbury, who remained evasive, the conclusion of a military agreement to restrain Russia from taking action. Crispi was the very man for Bismarck who, to flatter him and persuade him to cooperate with Austria and England in the Near East, invited him to talks at Friedrichsruhe on 2 and 3 October. On returning from Friedrichsruhe Crispi assured the Austrian Ambassador at Rome that if Russia attacked Turkey or invaded Bulgaria Italy would aid Austria with 100,000 or 200,000 men. He accepted with alacrity an eight-point program agreed upon by the Austrian, British, and Italian Ambassadors at Constantinople to safeguard the Near Eastern interests of the three powers. He even sought to extend the scope of point VIII and to specify what action was to be taken if Turkey broke up, as might happen from one minute to the next. But Bismarck and Kalnoky were not prepared to go so far as that.

British acceptance of this program, which extended the Anglo-Italian Mediterranean understanding of 12 February 1887 to cover the Near East and concerned Austria particularly, was obtained by Bismarck who on 22 November wrote a personal letter to Salisbury to plead in its favor, revealing the 1879 treaty with Austria to him so as to reassure him on German policy and convince him that Austria had Germany behind her. The eight (ultimately nine) points of the program were laid down in an exchange of notes on 12 December 1887 between Karoly, the Austrian ambassador in London, and Salisbury, the Italian signature being given in Vienna by Nigra on 16 December. The nine points dealt with the maintenance of

(1) peace; (2) the *status quo* and (3) the local autonomies; (4) the independence of Turkey and the freedom of the Straits; (5) a veto on Turkey's ceding or delegating her suzerain rights over Bulgaria to another power; (6) the desire of the three powers to associate Turkey with the defense of these principles; (7) their agreement on the measures to be taken if Turkey failed to resist some illegal enterprise; (8) the provisional occupation of points of Ottoman territory mutually agreed upon if the Porte connived at any illegal enterprise; (9) the secrecy to be observed on the agreement. This agreement, which aimed at restraining Russia from invading Bulgaria and bringing pressure to bear on Turkey, fulfilled its purpose without the need for active measures.

In January 1888 the Italo-German military convention was concluded for which Crispi had expressed a wish in his talk with Bismarck at Friedrichsruhe. By it the Italian General Staff engaged in case of a war of the Triplice Powers with France and Russia, to attack France in the Alps with the main part of its forces and send to the Rhine via Austria-Hungary approximately six army corps and three cavalry divisions. Austria-Hungary reserved the right not to give passage to troops across her territory if the war were localized between Germany and Italy on the one side and France on the other. On the other hand, no decision was taken as to Italo-Austrian military cooperation against Russia, offered by Crispi to the Ambassador Bruck, because Kalnoky feared that Italy would ask for territory of the monarchy in return. Kalnoky in March 1889 also declined Crispi's proposal for a naval agreement, pretexting that the two fleets would have to operate in different parts of the Mediterranean, and he would not consider proposals for a naval and military convention which Crispi sent by Nigra in August 1889.

Austria, too, towards the end of 1887 would have liked to open discussions with Germany, in order to clarify the conditions in which the *casus foederis* would arise and decide on the exact distribution of the forces of the two countries in the event of war with Russia, regarded in the spring of 1888 as inevitable. The German General Staff which disapproved of Bismarck's policy and wanted a preventive war to forestall Russian preparations would gladly have seconded the Austrian move. But Bismarck, who would do nothing to encourage Austria-Hungary to provoke a conflict with Russia

and was convinced that Russia, powerless as she was, would not
be the aggressor, remained firm in his opposition.

The ebullience of the Magyar magnates was cooled and the eyes
of the Russian nationalists were opened by the publication on 3
February 1888 of the 1879 treaty between Germany and Austria-
Hungary, followed three days later by a great speech by Bismarck
in the Reichstag in which he spoke in forthright terms of the great
service he had rendered to Russia in 1878 at the Congress of Berlin
and of the ingratitude he had reaped, forcing him into an alliance
with Austria-Hungary first and later with Italy. It was in this famous
speech that the chancellor uttered the words: "We Germans fear
God and naught else in the world and it is the fear of God that
makes us love and foster peace." But this maneuvering between
Russia on one side and Austria-Hungary, Italy, and Britain on the
other grew daily more difficult. "Laissez-nous en tête-à-tête avec
l'Autriche; voilà tout ce que nous demandons" was, as reported
from St. Petersburg on 9 October 1888 the Russian refrain annotated
by Bismarck with the words: "Et après?" meaning: what would happen if he did allow this? His policy had always been to remain true
to the overriding principle of calming down conflicts between the
various powers and maintaining peace in the supreme interest of
Germany. Wilhelm I once said to him: "I would not be in your shoes.
You seem to me at times to be like a rider who juggles on horseback
with five balls, never letting one fall."

William L. Langer

THE DIPLOMACY OF CHECKS AND BALANCES

The works of William L. Langer of Harvard University are indispensable for
an understanding of European diplomacy during the last decades of the
nineteenth century. They present a careful historical synthesis based on
familiarity with a vast body of primary materials and secondary accounts in

Reprinted from *European Alliances and Alignments, 1871–1890*, 2nd ed., pp. 451–
453, 503–505, by William L. Langer, by permission of Alfred A. Knopf, Inc. Copyright
1931, 1950 by Alfred A. Knopf, Inc.

several languages. Langer has been criticized on some points, especially for his undisguised admiration of Bismarck's conduct of foreign affairs. But his views are supported by solid research, and while they should not be accepted as infallible, neither can they be rejected out of hand. Nowhere did the Iron Chancellor's extraordinary ability appear to greater advantage than in his mastery of diplomacy.

A more complicated chapter of diplomacy than that dealing with the year 1887 could hardly be found in the history of European international relations. And yet, though the clouds of war lowered on all horizons, the general peace was maintained. This fact alone is a tribute to the statesmen of the continent, most of whom desired to avoid conflict and showed but little sympathy with the violent outbursts of national sentiment or the pressure for action exerted by the military men. But it may well be doubted whether the statesmen could have held their own against such pressure had it not been for the mastery with which Bismarck guided the course of diplomacy. It is easy enough to understand that many political and military writers of the time regarded him as an evil spirit, a demon, an intriguer, a bully. They could not know what was going on behind the scenes, for the agreements made in this eventful year were secret. Had the chancellor had his way, they would probably have been public, as public as his great speeches, in which he reviewed the situation with the greatest bluntness, not to say brutality. Bismarck believed in an open diplomacy supported by strong national forces. He did not allow the military power of Germany to fall behind that of her neighbors, but he did not intend to use Germany's power for aggressive purposes. For him Germany was a "saturated" nation, forced to maintain a strong military establishment because of her dangerous geographical location.

As for his diplomacy, it was really simple in its underlying principles, and anyone might have understood it. Threatened on two fronts, Germany's interest was to prevent the formation of a Franco-Russian coalition by showing herself amenable to Russian desires in Bulgaria, where Germany had no direct interests. The difficulty with this solution, however, arose from the fact that the Austrians and the Russians would not agree to a peaceful partition of the Balkans into spheres of influence. They threatened to go to war over the Bulgarian question. Now it was clear that in a Russian-Austrian conflict one of two things would happen. Either Russia would attack, in which event Germany would be brought in on Austria's side under the terms of the alliance of 1879; or Austria would attack and most likely be defeated unless Germany came to her assistance. But Germany could not afford to see the position of Austria as a great power jeopardized by a Russian victory. How was the dilemma to be solved? The Reinsurance Treaty is the key to the whole situation, for in it Bismarck, while securing Germany against the danger of a Franco-Russian alliance, checkmated the two eastern powers: Germany would stand by the party attacked. Thereby, as Bismarck put it, he had set a premium upon the preservation of peace.

There was only one great danger that haunted Bismarck after the conclusion of the Reinsurance Treaty, and that was that Russia, counting on German neutrality if Austria were the aggressor, would provoke the latter into taking the initiative. What would Germany's position then be? This difficulty was to be solved by the Mediterranean coalition, which in its earlier form was to ensure the three powers, England, Austria, and Italy, against the disturbance of the *status quo* in the Mediterranean. The agreement of December 12 represented a great reinforcement of the earlier understanding and made Russian action in the east almost impossible. She could no longer provoke Austria without coming to blows with the Near Eastern Triplice. Quite naturally, she chose to retreat in the Bulgarian question.

In all this there was no question of loyalty or disloyalty on Bismarck's part, any more than there was a question of his siding with one power as against another. Historians who attempt to make out a case of this sort in one way or the other are bound to find themselves in a blind alley. The German chancellor repeatedly distinguished between a policy of interests and a policy of prestige. He was following the interests of Germany, nothing more, nothing less. But above all he based his policy upon real factors in European relations. He did not expect others to act contrary to their own interests. Just as he would not engage Germany in a quarrel with Russia over Bulgaria or take the side of Austria in a Balkan policy which did not concern Germany, so he avoided unreasonable demands upon other powers. If the Austrians wished to fight because of Bulgaria, well and good, but let them first assure themselves of the proper support. Did the English wish to smash the Franco-Russian coalition in the Egyptian question and resist the Russian policy in the east at all costs? Let them do so, but let them first make the necessary arrangements with Austria and Italy, countries which had similar interests. In the same way the Italians should enlist the aid of the other Mediterranean powers if they hoped to check the French policy in North Africa.

One can hardly escape the conviction that Bismarck throughout this critical year, while doing his utmost to liberate Germany from the danger of a Franco-Russian alliance, at the same time maintained a careful balance between the other powers. He deluded and disappointed some and enraged others, Austrians as well as French and Russians, but he preserved the peace. Had he not been there, the nations would have had it out in the good old way. They had often fought on less pretext. But for Germany's sake Bismarck desired to avoid any conflict in Europe. He would not fight himself, no matter how favorable the situation might be for Germany, but at the same time he would not let the others fight if he could help it. As the situation stood at the end of 1887, no power could move without involving itself in endless difficulties and dangers. The sanctions of peace lay in the great alliance system which spread over Europe like a huge web. Bismarck was denounced and misunderstood, but for him the preservation of peace was worth it. . . .

His had been a great career, beginning with three wars in eight years and ending with a period of twenty years during which he worked for the peace of Europe, despite countless opportunities to embark on further enterprises with more than an even chance of success. No other statesman of his standing had ever before shown the same great moderation and sound political sense of the possible and the desirable. Of course much had changed since the time when he first took over the control of Prussian policy, and it cannot be said that he succeeded entirely in estimating the new forces at their full value. In the last years of his régime the old cabinet diplomacy had become quite impossible, for the dissemination of education and more liberal representative institutions had made public opinion a force in foreign affairs. Bismarck himself had not been much influenced by this new factor, for the German Reichstag had little to say in matters of international relations, and the chancellor, with his "reptile fund," was able to mold press opinion to suit his needs, especially in cases of army appropriations. He had a very keen appreciation of the strength and danger of popular passions in other countries, but he was often unwise and unscrupulous in the way in which he manipulated German opinion and aroused the feelings of other nations.

It might also be said that the great chancellor failed to understand all the implications of the great economic changes that were taking place in Europe. The technical advances in armaments he saw clearly enough and he had no hesitation in joining the race for military power without making any serious effort to check the disastrous development of a Europe armed to the teeth. But his advocacy of a colonial policy was hardly more than reluctant and half-hearted. Even though he realized the growing importance of overseas sources and markets, he was, to the end, primarily a continental statesman. In the same way he allowed himself to be carried away by the wave of protection that swept Europe towards the end of the century, yet without seeing the great importance of close economic connections between Germany and her allies, let alone countries like Russia. The force of international finance escaped him almost completely until the very last years of his chancellorship, and by that time it was almost too late to check the course of events.

It must be remembered, of course, that no other statesman of his time was able to grasp the full significance of these tremendous changes. Bismarck at least deserves full credit for having steered European politics through this dangerous transitional period without serious conflict between the great powers. Paradoxically enough it may be said that by preserving the peace of Europe the great chancellor made possible the phenomenal development of forces which made peace more and more difficult to maintain in the future. As for his own diplomacy, its methods changed while its purposes remained the same. In 1871 he was certainly an advocate of the free hand in international relations. To bind oneself beforehand for certain eventualities that might never occur seemed to him contrary to the fundamental principles of good statesmanship. And yet when he laid down his offices, he had built up the most complicated system of alliances that Europe had ever known in peace times. It was, of course, the product of circumstances, the resultant of the new forces and the new pressure in international relations.

What his alliances came to in the aggregate was a series of security pacts designed to protect the German Empire from any conceivable attack so far as human foresight and ingenuity could do so. With the exception of a slight nuance in the German-Italian treaty of 1887 these agreements were all strictly defensive and were intended to secure the European center from aggression by the wings. To say that Bismarck's object was to isolate France is only a simplification of his policy and a half-truth. His object was to reduce the pressure upon the German frontiers as much as possible by diverting the European powers to colonial fields and by building up a system of protective agreements that made action difficult and dangerous. Realizing full well that the ferment and urge for expansion in a nation like Russia could not be wholly suppressed, he was willing to protect the Russian rear while the Russians were busy in Asia. He was willing even to allow them a reasonable field for expansion in the eastern Balkans. It was only because Austria, which was absolutely necessary to Germany to complete the Central European dike against Russia, objected to Russian activity even in Bulgaria that the German chancellor was led into the policy of the Mediterranean coalition. This combination, as viewed from Berlin, was designed for the simple purpose, not of checking the Russian advance in the Near East, for which Bismarck cared nothing, but of securing for Austria the support of England and Italy in protecting interests for which Germany was unwilling to fight. It was the classic illustration of Bismarck's uncanny sense for the objects and interests of other nations as well as of Germany. The Mediterranean coalition was a tool in Bismarck's hand, but it was not based on unfair exploitation of the other powers. Quite the contrary, the chancellor simply brought together powers like England and Austria who had been for years groping in the dark to join hands.

V THE IRON CHANCELLOR

C. Grant Robertson
THE STRUGGLE OF CHURCH AND STATE

One of the best biographies of Bismarck in English is still the one by Charles Grant Robertson which appeared soon after the First World War. It is lively and perceptive, and while the author did not have access to the archives which the Weimar Republic opened to scholars in the 1920s, his conclusions are by and large sound. During his years at Oxford and the University of Birmingham Robertson wrote voluminously on the history of Europe, but none of his works has withstood the passage of time as well as his study of the Iron Chancellor. In the selection which follows he describes the course and outcome of the Kulturkampf.

Bismarck's decision to crush the Clerical Center was momentous. After 1878 he argued that he was not responsible for the policy of the *Kulturkampf,* nor for the May Laws and their execution. The argument will not stand the test of facts nor of probability. In 1872, 1873, and 1875 he spoke repeatedly both in the Reichstag and the Prussian Landtag in defense of the coercive legislation and of the general policy of Prussia and the empire in the controversy. He complained bitterly in private letters to Roon of the desertion of the Conservative Party in the "Catholic controversy"; he was responsible for the appointment of Falk, and supported him until 1878 against the attacks in Court circles. It is, in the absence of all corroborative evidence to the contrary, impossible to believe that Bismarck as chancellor and minister-president would have allowed a subordinate colleague to embark Prussia and the empire by legislation and administrative action in a life-and-death struggle, which involved the most delicate and fundamental issues of high policy at home and abroad, without his complete concurrence. It is demonstrable that the correspondence between the emperor and the pope, which stated very tersely the Prussian attitude, was on the emperor's side drafted by Bismarck; the withdrawal of the German mission from the Curia—the rupture, in fact, of diplomatic relations—was Bismarck's act, and in the negotiations after 1878 Bismarck assumed that the May Laws would not be withdrawn unless the Vatican made substantial concessions. The

From C. Grant Robertson, *Bismarck* (New York, 1919), pp. 328–333, 337–338. Reprinted by permission of Constable & Co. Ltd. and Howard Fertig, Inc.

later assertion (in 1878 and repeated in his Memoirs) that he regarded the struggle as mainly a recrudescence of the chronic problem of Poland was an afterthought, and the blame subsequently laid on Falk, as the author of the mischief and the failure, was a characteristic trait of ingratitude. A scapegoat had to be found, and Falk, the hero of the National Liberals and Radicals, served the convenient purpose of exculpating the chancellor and affronting the parties with which Bismarck broke between 1878 and 1879.

In 1874 Bismarck told the Reichstag that since 1862 his previsions and forecasts in all the great issues had been wonderfully accurate. The remark had a side reference to the *Kulturkampf*. But in 1871 Bismarck plainly miscalculated. The diplomacy with which he had hitherto crossed swords successfully had not had the traditions, skill, fertility in resource, and pertinacity of the Vatican. The Roman Curia could and did pull many wires throughout Europe, and it could afford to wait. It had no capital that could be stormed, leaving the defense impotent. Its capital was everywhere, planted in the consciences of millions of its communion. Heads can be cut off, but the obedience of heart and will cannot be enforced by prison or the guillotine. Bullets or wristcuffs cannot kill ideas. The extermination of the faithful is not the same thing as the extirpation of a faith. Indeed, the seven years from 1871 to 1878 were an instructive object lesson in the limits of power even when exercised by a state with the executive strength of Prussia. In the constitutional conflict of 1862 Bismarck had rightly assumed that the Liberals would not raise barricades, defy the laws, or refuse to pay taxes, and that, if they did, the whiff of grapeshot would settle the first outbreak. In 1872 he apparently calculated that the Catholics would either not resist, or, if they did, would soon surrender to a rigorous coercion. He was completely mistaken. When cardinal archbishops, with the applause of their congregations, defied the law and went to prison, the state as power could only, as Windthorst remarked, bring in the guillotine— if it dared. For when a state by its own action converts law-breakers into martyrs for conscience it loses the sympathy of the law-abiding. The average German began to think as Pepys did when he saw oppressed Dissenters going to prison under the Clarendon code: "I would to God they would conform or not be so well catch'd." Universal suffrage proved a terrible weapon in the hands of the Center

Party. At the general election of 1874 the National Liberals increased their numbers to over one hundred and fifty, but the Clericals polled a million and a half votes and returned not sixty but ninety-one members. Bismarck therefore had to face a National Liberal Party stronger than ever and more indispensable to the government, and a Center opposition enormously encouraged by its success.

It was in the nature of things that on both sides the struggle should extend far beyond the limits foreseen in 1871: and the simple original issue, whether the Vatican should or should not constrain opponents of the decrees to obedience, was by 1876 converted into an illimitable controversy on the functions, basis, character, and ends of civil government and its relation to ecclesiastical authority; it threatened to divide Germany into two great confessional camps, Protestant and Catholic, and to throw back the newly born empire of 1871 into the maelstrom of Charles V and the epoch of the Reformation, with the passions of medieval Guelph and Ghibelline, and of empire and papacy superimposed. In the welter of conflict the secession and formation of the "Old Catholics," a tiny handful of the combatants, became a neglected by-issue. The fiery support of religious and political Protestantism, and of the powerful secularist intellectuals who desired to see a complete separation of church and state in every German state, and the extirpation of denominational endowment and teaching, was fatal to Liberal Catholicism. The issues raised by Vaticanism became an assault in many quarters on the Roman Catholic Church: and the cry of "Los von Rom" and the establishment of a German national Catholic Church on Febronian lines, independent of the papacy, aided the papal effort to represent "the May Laws," as a Diocletian persecution, led by Bismarck into whom Satan had entered.

To the papacy, indeed, the *Kulturkampf* proved to be an unqualified blessing. In 1871 and 1872 the antiinfallibility movement within the Roman Communion was a grave danger. But with an unerring eye the directors of Vatican policy seized the weapon of their adversaries and turned it against them. They closed the Roman Catholic ranks as far as possible, and shifted the issue from the narrower field of "the May Laws" to a trial of strength between the Roman Church as a whole and its opponents spiritual or secular. The more eagerly did those opponents mass for attacks on a broad front, the broader the front on which the Vatican deployed its counterattacks. Windthorst proved himself a consummate tactician and a polished debater. He placed large issues in sonorous phrases before the electorate in the program of the Clerical Center—freedom of conscience, the independence of religion, the liberty of the individual German to worship as reason led him, an empire based on justice *(justitia fundamentum regnorum),* taken from the medieval law books—and by provocative taunts he understood how to seduce Conservatives, Liberals, Radicals, and Progressives into violent indiscretions. It required courage to stand up to Bismarck, but Windthorst smilingly removed the gloves and took and gave telling punishment with a finished equanimity.

The results by 1878 were disquieting. Lord Odo Russell's dispatches from 1873–1877 indicate Bismarck's depression, irritation, and anxiety. The Clericals had built up a powerful and extraordinarily well-organized party; they had ample funds, an influential press, and a network of local machinery. It was the *Kulturkampf* which enabled the Center to become in Bismarck's lifetime the best drilled, most obedient, and strongest single party in Germany. They drew their strength from every class—from cardinals and Polish magnates to the industrial democracy in the old ecclesiastical principalities. The stronger the executive action against them, the stronger they reacted against it. The disciplining of Germany for two generations told immensely in their favor. The Clericals, and later the Social Democrats, had in the German voter a man who had been drilled in a great military machine, to whom obedience to command was life. Given an organizer, a party with a real cause had organizable material ready to hand in the German electorate. The Roman Church was an organization already made. Windthorst enjoyed its matchless and unlimited support. The decadence of National Liberalism after 1878 is largely accounted for by the absence of an intelligible cause, the halting and contradictory language of its spokesmen, and its dependence on a reservoir in a single social stratum, the middle class. The Clerical Party had none of these patent defects.

The ministerial conduct of the fight was vitiated also by serious blunders. The punitive measures against the inferior clergy—the hard-working priest of the village and small town—threw hundreds of parishes, ignorant of the deeper issues of Vaticanism, into opposition. The government made no effort to enlist the sympathy of educated Catholicism with the cause of freedom of opinion. Instead of concentrating on the narrower issue of Vaticanism and assisting the German hierarchy, placed in a grave perplexity between two allegiances and influenced by a genuine antipathy to the more profound consequences in the decrees and by a patriotic reluctance to defy the law binding on German citizens; instead of trying to find a compromise for the bishops coerced by Rome and menaced by the state; instead of rallying the Catholic laity to the support of its episcopate in the struggle with the Curia, the government struck right and left at high and low with the indiscrimination of brute strength. Falk fought with the ability of a trained lawyer who assumes that a juristic answer, expressed in well-drafted legislation, and backed by executive action, can settle every problem of life and conduct. Bismarck left the law to Falk, the administration to the Home Office, and thought of the higher politics alone. The limitations in his statecraft were at once exposed. This was not a case where "one hand could wash the other." The subtle yet deep intellectual and moral implications in the controversy did not interest him, nor had he the time, the inclination, or the accumulated knowledge to master them. And, as with Napoleon I in his struggle with the papacy, the ingrained contempt for ideas as ideas, for "idealogues," and for men to whom ideas have a more inspiring import than material force warped his judgment and blinded his intuition. To Bismarck, as to Napoleon, the church was a necessity of an ordered life, but its action and position must be strictly correlated to the ends prescribed by reasons of state. In the *Kulturkampf* Bismarck found himself in deeper water than his strength and skill could manage. . . .

It is commonly said that the Bismarckian policy in the *Kulturkampf* ended in a complete defeat—proved by the recantation of the next ten years. Three comments, however, are essential in this connection. First, the Liberal parties which passed and upheld "the May Laws" and the principles underlying them never recanted nor repented. On the contrary, they opposed and lamented, with good reason, the chancellor's surrender. Secondly, the Vatican in 1878 was as tired of the struggle as Bismarck. It had not been defeated, but it had failed so far to secure amendment, much less repeal, of "the May Laws." By 1878 the danger of serious schism within the Roman

Communion had vanished. Ninety-nine Catholics out of a hundred accepted the Vatican Decrees, but the Roman Church in Germany was crippled by the Falk code. Had the National Liberals come into office, determined to fight to a finish, the Vatican would not have had an alliance to sell which gave it so commanding a position in the negotiations that followed the death of Pio Nono and the accession of Leo XIII. There is every reason to suppose that a strong National Liberal ministry could have continued the struggle and imposed a very different compromise to that dictated from Rome and accepted by Bismarck. Thirdly, Bismarck deliberately sacrificed victory in the *Kulturkampf* to victory in other issues, more important in his judgment.

Johannes Ziekursch

THE CAMPAIGN AGAINST SOCIALISM

Few German academicians spoke out during the 1920s in defense of the ill-fated Weimar Republic. This reluctance of the intellectual leaders of the country to commit themselves to the democratic ideal contributed to its decline. But there was nothing pusillanimous about the stand taken by Johannes Ziekursch, professor of history at the Universities of Breslau and Cologne. His spirited account of the German Empire reveals a firm faith in the liberal creed. It charges Bismarck with the sins of authoritarianism and arbitrariness which brought the nation to disaster in 1918. The vain struggle against socialism, it maintains, reveals the Iron Chancellor's reliance on the mailed fist in dealing with those he could not cajole or frighten.

In the Reichstag elections of January 1877 the number of Social Democratic votes rose by 40 percent, from 352,000 in 1874 to 493,000. Only the National Liberals, the Center, and the Conservatives showed greater strength. To seven Saxon electoral districts and one Thuringian were added two in Berlin, one in Silesia, and one in the Rhine-

From Johannes Ziekursch, *Politische Geschichte Des Neuen Deutschen Kaiserreiches*, 3 vols. (Frankfurt am Main, 1925–1930), II: 325–333. Reprinted by permission of Frankfurter Societäts-Druckerei G.m.b.H. Translated by Theodore S. Hamerow and William W. Beyer.

land. The number of Socialist Party newspapers grew from year to year with surprising rapidity. In 1878 there were already 75 of them, both large and small.

As early as the imperial press law of 1874 and the penal law of 1875 Bismarck had demanded weapons against this party, but without success. Nine days after Hödel's attempt on the life of the Kaiser an anti-Socialist bill was presented to the Reichstag at the insistence of the chancellor. The Free Conservative Minister of Agriculture Friedenthal and the Conservative Minister of Justice Leonhardt had vainly warned against the promulgation of an exceptional law. The effect of such laws during the *Kulturkampf* had been apparent to all. But Bismarck replied that

> we can only strike at the heart of Social Democracy if we are empowered to disregard the barriers which the (Prussian) constitution has established in the so-called fundamental rights, barriers arising out of an excessive, doctrinaire concern for the protection of the individual and the parties. In dealing with Social Democracy the state must act in self-defense, and in self-defense one cannot be finicky in the choice of means.

Thus in a few days Privy Councilor Bucher in the Foreign Office drafted a law modeled after an English act of Parliament directed against the secret, revolutionary Irish Fenian Brotherhood. The law was very slipshod. Publications and associations pursuing the objectives of Social Democracy were to be prohibited, but the nature of these objectives was not clearly defined, so that, as Bennigsen pointed out in the Reichstag, even the most philanthropic activities and scholarly discussions could fall within this category. The Bundesrat, which met only from time to time and which voted according to instructions, was supposed to confirm or invalidate within four weeks every measure which the police had taken against Socialist publications, associations, and meetings. The decisions of the Bundesrat were to be considered by the Reichstag; 397 deputies of the most diverse political convictions, of whom only a fraction was trained in law, were then supposed to vote concerning the content, meaning, and danger of dozens of newspaper articles.

The National Liberal deputy from Leipzig Stephani concluded that the bill "is ostensibly directed against Social Democracy, but in fact against the National Liberals." "We are still not so frightened of the red specter," declared Hölder, a National Liberal from Württemberg, "as to sanction measures which we fought with all our strength when they were being promulgated by the late Diet of the German Confederation." On May 24, 1878, the Reichstag rejected the bill, after the National Liberals had declared themselves ready to support the government with an imperial law strengthening the provisions of state laws dealing with associations and assemblies. Even Bismarck's confidant, the head of his chancellery Privy Councilor von Tiedemann, admitted that the rejection of this anti-Socialist law was not unjustified.

Then on June 2, 1878, came a second attempt on the life of the Kaiser. An educated man of thirty, Dr. Karl Nobiling, the son of an estate manager in Posen, wounded the Kaiser so seriously that it was doubtful whether the octogenarian ruler would survive. For several months the crown prince had to take the place of his father. After his deed Nobiling tried to kill himself. Seriously wounded, he died three months later in prison. Nothing was known about any deposition he may have made, except that he was supposed to have subscribed to Socialist ideas.

When Bismarck in Friedrichsruhe received news of the assault, he exclaimed: "Now we will dissolve the Reichstag." He immediately reviewed all the political consequences of the attempted assassination, and only then inquired about the condition of the Kaiser and the details of the crime. He proposed to make good use of this unexpected incident.

The news of Nobiling's bloody assault on the monarch who had secured German unification and hegemony on the European continent after three glorious wars gave rise to wild indignation among the people. Rumors about attempts on the life of the crown prince and Prince Friedrich Karl, about plans to dynamite the palace in Berlin, and about the danger of a revolution in the capital flew about for the next few days. Monarchical loyalty and national pride condemned the ingratitude and public disgrace of Nobiling's outrage. Since both assassination attempts were immediately although mistakenly attributed to Social Democracy, popular anger turned against it. Feelings were intensified by fear of the dangerous forces of the underworld, which the public thought it had finally identified. Memories of the terrible days of the Paris Commune were awakened.

The economic ascendancy of the middle class since the founding of the Zollverein and the beginning of railroad construction had taken place in such a short time filled with great political struggles, and the economic difficulties of the last five years had been so serious, that the bourgeoisie had lacked the time and energy to concern itself with the condition of the industrial workers. The well-to-do found comfort in the doctrine of the harmony of economic life which alone would heal the injuries it had inflicted. They believed that government intervention in behalf of the workers could easily transform the economic crisis into a catastrophe. The workers were therefore urged to rely on their own strength and on the self-help to which the middle class owed its welfare, although under different conditions. Vainly had voices in the camp of the Clericals and the south German democrats appealed for social reforms. Vainly had after 1872 many scholars, the so-called "socialists of the chair," joined in the Association for Social Policy in order to awaken the public conscience and pave the way for reform by thorough scholarly research. The brusque, uncomprehending rejection of these efforts by Heinrich von Treitschke, the prophet of the German Empire, in his work on *Socialism and Its Patrons* exemplifies the attitude of the vast majority of the middle class. After the assassination attempts Treitschke's resounding condemnation of the Socialists seemed to most people entirely justified. The coarse, provocative tone which Socialist deputies, agitators, and newspapers had adopted in the past, and their constant threats of revolution now led to a terrible retribution.

Against the will of the majority of the Prussian ministry Bismarck forced the dissolution of the Reichstag, hoping to isolate the left wing of the National Liberals by intimidating the other members of the party. He rushed into the struggle not only against the Socialists, but also against the liberals. He let it be known everywhere that the Progressives could no longer be considered among the parties of order, and that there was no difference between voting for a Socialist and for a Progressive. Because of their occasional collaboration with the Progressives in elections the National Liberals were accused of indirect support of the Socialists. Then for the first time Bismarck began to think in earnest that a modification of the franchise or some change in the Reichstag and its constitutional position might be necessary. Not that he had until now considered the suffrage law inviolable. Almost immediately after its promulgation he had replied in the summer of 1867 to the warnings of district president von Diest in Wiesbaden: "If in a few years the system of election is no longer necessary, or if I do not like it any more, I will revoke it." The moment when he did not like it any more was about to come. On August 12, 1878, Bismarck wrote the King of Bavaria:

> *The purpose of the German Empire is the maintenance of justice. At the time of the establishment of the existing union of princes and cities parliamentary activity was envisioned as a means of achieving the purpose of the federation, not as an end in itself. I hope that the conduct of the (new) Reichstag will spare the associated state governments the need ever to act on the practical implications of this legal situation.*

Besides the destruction of the Socialists, Bismarck demanded of the new Reichstag completion of the reform of imperial finances which was supposed to end contributions from the states and even provide a considerable surplus for them. In Prussia the lowest brackets of the class tax yielding 21 million marks, which in the days of the economic crisis could in most cases be collected only by the bailiff, were to be eliminated, while half of the land and property tax amounting to 35 million marks was to be transferred to the municipalities. The trade tax paid by artisans and small shopkeepers was to be reduced by 2.5 million marks. Hobrecht, the new Prussian minister of finance, privately demanded an additional 60 million marks for other purposes. Thus for Prussia the new system would have to provide altogether about 120 million marks, for the other federal states 80 million, and for the empire 45 million, so that the reform was to bring in approximately a quarter of a billion marks. With such hopes and promises did the government enter the election campaign which was decided at the end of July and in August 1878.

In the election 360,000 more voters went to the polls than in the preceding year. The Socialists, nevertheless, lost 56,000 votes or 11.3 percent of their total vote of 1877, while the National Liberals lost 150,000 votes or 10.4 percent, the Progressives and the Löwe faction 35,000 or 7 percent, and the Center 27,000 or 2 percent. The Conservatives gained 219,000 votes or 41.9 percent of the votes they polled in 1877, and the Reich Party gained 366,000 votes or 86.3 percent.

Accordingly the National Liberals declined from 127 to 98 seats, the Progressives and the Löwe faction from 44 to 31, and the Socialists from 12 to 9, while the Center suffered no losses and even increased its representation when its Guelph allies grew from 4 to 10. The Conservatives increased from 40 to 59 seats, and the Reich Party from 38 to 56. Now 129 liberals opposed 115 conservatives and 103 Clericals and Guelphs. The decisive role was no longer played by the liberals but by the conservatives, who could combine with either the liberals or the Center. Despite his opposition to the National Liberals before the election, Bismarck invited them afterward to collaborate with the conservatives.

A much improved version of the anti-Socialist law was submitted to the new Reichstag. For example, appeals against police measures were no longer to be submitted to the Bundesrat and the Reichstag, but to a commission composed of four members of the Bundesrat and five judges under a chairman appointed by the Kaiser. Socialist meetings, parades, celebrations, and associations could be prohibited. Professional agitators who had violated the law might be expelled by court order from specified towns and districts, but expulsion from their place of domicile was to be legal only if they had resided there less than six months. Those agitators who were innkeepers, printers, booksellers, and lending librarians could be barred from practicing their occupation, while in districts exposed to danger martial law might be proclaimed. Furthermore, all meetings had to be approved in advance by the police, the sale of publications on the streets and the possession of arms could be prohibited, and persons who presumably endangered public safety could be exiled.

The premature disclosure of the draft of the anti-Socialist law deprived Bismarck of the chance to add even more rigorous restrictions. He wanted, for example, the right to dismiss Socialist civil servants without a pension, for he clearly recognized that

> the majority of the poorly paid minor officials in Berlin, and then the railroad signalman, the switchman, and similar categories are Socialists, a situation whose dangers may become evident in times of insurrection and in the transportation of troops. I believe, moreover, that if the law is

to be effective, then it is impossible in the long run to allow any citizen legally proved a Socialist to retain the suffrage, the right to run for office, and the enjoyment of the privileges of a member of the Reichstag.

Bismarck therefore came to the conclusion that "the bill as it now stands does no serious harm to socialism, and is altogether inadequate for its suppression."

At Lasker's suggestion the Reichstag limited the law to two and a half years, until the end of March 1881. Thereby the measure lost much of its effectiveness, while provoking the workers by the repeated debates in the Reichstag concerning its renewal. Because of this and other shortcomings Bismarck might perhaps have ordered another dissolution of the Reichstag, if the crown prince, who was still acting in the place of his sick father, had not opposed the plan. On October 19, 1878, the anti-Socialist law was passed by the votes of the Conservatives, the Reich party, the National Liberals, and the Löwe faction.

All the political parties had taken the same position as at the time of the first anti-Socialist law. Only the National Liberals and the supporters of Löwe had yielded to the pressure of popular excitement after the assassination attempts. The National Liberals understood the significance of their about-face. Their *Korrespondenz* wrote at the time:

No one fails to recognize that the suppression of revolutionary aspirations will not be without effect on civic freedom in general. As long as we are engaged in a struggle against the Socialist mortal enemy, any further development of the constitutional state can certainly not be considered.

Such was the end of the confident belief which had prevailed since 1866 that political unity had to be achieved first, because then the liberal development of the empire would inevitably follow. With the anti-Socialist law the liberal bourgeoisie rejected the workers, just as it had completely embittered the Catholics by the *Kulturkampf,* and provoked the Conservatives through the reform of the Prussian administration without weakening them. The liberal era ended at about the same time that Bismarck thought he had won leadership among the European Great Powers at the Congress of Berlin. For he felt that he could finally dispense with the support in domestic affairs on which he had hitherto relied. The anti-Socialist law thrust a thorn into the flesh of the German people; a festering wound was opened which still has not healed to the present time.

William Harbutt Dawson
THE TURN FROM LAISSEZ FAIRE

Although he entitled his major work The German Empire, 1867–1914, and the Unity Movement, *William Harbutt Dawson devoted the bulk of it to Bismarck. He had met the Iron Chancellor while pursuing his studies on the Continent, and the tough old statesman made a lasting impression on the English scholar. The works he wrote were designed to provide his countrymen with a better understanding of the political and economic life of Germany. He was particularly interested in the attempt to protect the lower classes against hard times by a system of social insurance, since the problems created by industrialism in Great Britain were similar to those with which Bismarck had had to deal in the 1880s.*

When the question of social reform was taken up in earnest it was on the initiative of a minister who hitherto had not touched and had barely looked at it. Bismarck had, indeed, already shown in his own crude way that he was not insensible to the sufferings of the poorer classes. Visiting England in 1862 he heard of the success of the cooperative movement, and on his return home he interested the King of Prussia in the movement. When a little later Lassalle came forward with his project of productive associations on a cooperative basis he persuaded the king to make a grant from his privy purse towards the cost of forming societies. Owing to his influence also the Silesian handloom weavers in 1865 received from the same source help in starting a cooperative manufactory. All this may have been laudable benevolence, but it was not social reform. Years were to pass before Bismarck realized that social conditions required ameliorative legislation. Busch, strong on the motives and origins of

From William Harbutt Dawson, *The German Empire, 1867–1914, and the Unity Movement,* 2 vols. (New York, 1919), II: 39–46. Reprinted by permission of George Allen & Unwin Ltd.

Bismarckian policies, says that he awakened to the recognition of a social question as early as 1871, when exchanging ideas with European governments regarding the measures best suited to counteract the Internationalist movement. If he awakened, he did no more at that time, for it was his struggle with socialism at home, which began seven years later, that really opened his eyes to the fact that all could not be well with the social system under which hundreds of thousands of the most patient people in the world were flocking to the banner inscribed "Proletarians of all countries, unite!"

Was Bismarck ever a social reformer by study and reasoned conviction? It is doing him no injustice to answer this question negatively. Upon this, as most questions, he was guided by intuition and instinct. He saw that things were wrong, and without troubling about scientific theories and sanctions, he tried, by heroic measures and straight cuts, to make them right. Yet his solicitude for the working classes was an acquired solicitude, and he arrived at it under the pressure of political difficulties. The whole bent of his mind was against any interference with the "natural" relations of capital and labor. When, as late as 1877, the Prussian minister of commerce prepared a bill which was intended to afford to the working classes greater protection in matters affecting their physical and moral welfare, Bismarck criticized it so severely that it had to be dropped. He regarded the labor question still as essentially one of more or less wages, of longer or shorter hours of employment, and he was far more concerned that employers should not be unduly crippled in their power to meet labor's just demands than that work should be done under ideal conditions. For traces of any genuine comprehension of social problems, or even of intimate knowledge of the working classes, Bismarck's speeches will be searched in vain. They abound in vivid intuitions of economic truth, in true and sagacious reflections upon social relations, and invaluable *dicta* of common sense and worldly wisdom, which even the best trained sociologist may still read with profit, but they reflect a mind influenced rather by expediency than deep conviction and impelling enthusiasm. He passed social laws because they were necessary; social reform was never to him a passion, but always a policy.

When, however, Bismarck had once decided to enter this untried path, progress was far easier for him than it was for the early reformers in England, where the prejudices and preconceptions to be overcome were so many and so deeply rooted. Individualism seemed to have conquered in Germany, but the truth was that the victory had merely been that of the handful of men who had for the time controlled fiscal and economic policy in the ministries, and it lasted only so long as they lasted. Never did individualism obtain a firm hold upon national thought. The theory that the state had an unquestionable right to interfere in any direction in which the common good was endangered, and that it was the special duty of the crown to hold the balance between conflicting interests, had for generations been a ruling tradition of Prussian statecraft. Now, in the conditions incidental to a time of transition, this tradition proved of immense value. It was not necessary to create precedents for state action; precedents existed in abundance, and all that was needed was to go back to the forsaken ways.

The student who compares the different lines followed by social movements, particularly as reflected in labor law reforms, in England and Germany will find an invaluable clue in the fact that these movements have relied for their chief impetus in one country upon self-help and in the other upon state initiative and furtherance. In England the tendency was to set labor free from fetters and then leave it to fight its own battles. Hence freedom to organize in trade unions was given to the English working classes as early as 1825. In Germany the tendency was the other way. There labor has never yet been free, and such liberty of action as it enjoys today was gained in England half a century ago. To governments still steeped in the traditions of absolutism it seemed safer to admit a tacit obligation to do for labor what it was not able or allowed to do for itself. That labor has so seldom given proof of gratitude for the boons conferred upon it is chiefly due to the fact that the state has never seriously tried to view labor questions from the labor standpoint, and that reforms for its benefit have too often been carried out only under pressure. "While we laud and magnify the great deeds of the Imperial government in social politics," writes a German historian of social movements, Dr. F. Naumann, "it must never be forgotten that many of the great deeds were only necessary because of the gigantic blunders of the same government, and that all the laws for the protection of skilled workmen are a poor substitute for the free activity of the trade unions."

Inheriting these traditions, Bismarck decided before the empire was ten years old to embark upon the largest and most original experiment in constructive social reform ever attempted, an experiment which threw into the shade the best that had been done by the heavy-handed but well-meaning patriarchalism of the past. Brushing on one side all questions of wages and hours of labor, as questions which the working classes should be left to settle with their employers, and ignoring all demands for the right of free organization and combination, as opening up a vista of dangerous possibilities at a time when Socialistic doctrines were making ominous headway, he proposed a great scheme of social insurance by which the workers were to be afforded care and provision in all the vicissitudes of industrial life—medical treatment and maintenance in sickness, generous compensation in the event of accident, support during periods of unemployment, and finally pensions in the time of old age and permanent disablement.

The germ of this idea of social providence was to be found in existing institutions, some with a long and honorable past. Ever since the time of Frederick the Great there had been miners' benefit societies in Prussia, affording help to members and their dependents in times of need, societies so admirable in purpose and organization that all the modern insurance legislation has left them still free to do their old work in their own way. Since the middle of the century also societies for the relief of sickness had been formed in large numbers by the working classes on the voluntary principle which had already been successfully developed in England; in many parts of the country the same purpose was served by the workshop clubs, often subsidized by the employers; and in south Germany the municipalities insured the laboring classes against sickness. In spite of all these agencies, however, the number of wage-earners for whom such provision existed was still far smaller than the number of those without it.

One of the first measures passed by the Imperial Diet in 1871 had been an Employers' Liability Law, applying to factories, mines and quarries. Not only was that legislation partial, but liability was contingent on proof of culpability, and even more than the corresponding law of England it proved a fruitful source of litigation, engendering much bitterness. Often the injured workman's only chance of obtaining redress lay in appeal to the law court, where he fought against hopeless odds and under conditions which gave him every inducement to accept a fraction of his rights rather than risk the loss of the whole. On the other hand, the law was onerous and inequitable from the standpoint of small employers, since it made no provision for distributing the risks, with the result that these men often were either unable to meet their liabilities or were crushed beneath the weight of them.

A beginning was therefore made with the improvement of the provision for injured workmen. Instead of tinkering [with] the existing law, as was done later in England with deplorable results, Bismarck decided to legislate afresh upon the two principles of compulsory insurance and mutuality. The first Accident Insurance Bill was laid before the Diet in March 1881. It was intended to apply only to some of the more dangerous industries and enterprises and to secure almost automatically to the workpeople employed therein pensions for injuries which destroyed or reduced their earning capacity, with pensions to their dependents in the event of fatality. The employers were to pay two-thirds and the workpeople one-third of the premiums, and the state was to make a contribution towards increasing the benefits. Insurance was to be effected through a state institution with a view to eliminating private gain. Bismarck at once resolutely took the field on behalf of this social crusade, and during the five years occupied in passing the early insurance laws he expounded and defended his proposals at every step.

The only parties which took up an unfriendly attitude were the Social Democrats and the Radicals, the former because nothing short of the immediate realization of the collectivist state would satisfy them, the latter because the proposals were in conflict with their cherished individualistic doctrines. The Diet struck out the proposals for a Central Insurance Board and for state subsidies, and Bismarck withdrew the bill for the purpose of reconsidering both it and the Diet, for new elections were due in the autumn. In the hope of rallying the working classes to the support of the bill he now promised that part of the proceeds of a state tobacco monopoly, which he proposed simultaneously, should be applied towards the

cost of social reform, thus becoming a "patrimony for the disin-
herited." So confident was his belief in social reform as a political
asset that he appealed to the country mainly upon this question. The
issue was, however, complicated by the Protectionist controversy,
and the part of the nation which supported him on that question was
smaller than that which endorsed his social insurance policy. The result was that the ministerial parties lost many seats, and that for his
new majority Bismarck had to depend upon a coalition of Conservatives and Clericals.

The new Diet was opened on November 17th with a striking Imperial Message on the social question, since regarded as a classical
declaration of state policy towards labor, and still spoken of today as
the German charter of social reform. Emperor William I is commonly
credited, if not with the authorship, at least with the inspiration of
this memorable document. With neither authorship nor inspiration
had he anything whatever to do, for while it is true that it received
his cordial endorsement, as well as that of the crown prince, with
whom Bismarck conferred before its final form was decided, the
work itself, both in conception and composition, was his chancellor's. The Imperial Message was the precursor of a larger scheme
of social reform than had been contemplated hitherto; it was in
effect a declaration that social reform could never again be regarded
as a chapter of national life that could be completed by any specific
measures at any specific time, but must rather be thought of as
a running record of amelioration and progress, to which each generation and each decade must make its own due contribution.

It was not until June 1884, that a law on accident insurance was
passed. A larger group of trades and industries was embraced; the
principle of mutuality was retained; but the entire cost was now
placed upon the employers, who voluntarily renounced the offer
of a state subsidy rather than submit to the large measure of government interference which its acceptance would have entailed. The
law came into force on October 1, 1885, and during the succeeding
three years it was extended so as to include practically all the
wage-earning classes.

In the meantime a sickness insurance scheme had been enacted
on equally comprehensive lines. Introduced in the Diet in May 1882,
it was submitted to discussion and scrutiny for a whole year before

it was deemed fit to leave the legislature, so that when it became law in May 1883 (with force as from December 1, 1884), it was a masterly piece of constructive legislation, so thoroughly and honestly wrought in every part that it was able to stand the test of practice for a generation without any alteration of its main principles. The contributions required to meet the cost of benefits were to be paid to the extent of two-thirds by the workers and one-third by the employers; a state subsidy was neither given nor asked for.

Bismarck did not carry measures of such magnitude without encountering a vast amount of prejudice and much vehement hostility. Only two parties in the Diet carried their opposition to extremes— the Radicals on the plea that his reforms went too far, the Social Democrats on the plea that they did not go far enough. When Dr. Bamberger crystallized the objections of the former party in the dogmatic utterance, "To carry on social policy is to commit the state to a series of Socialistic postulates," Bismarck answered that he was too old to be terrified by phrases; it was enough for him that the policy which underlay his proposals, let these be called by whatever name the Radicals wished, was the traditional policy of Prussia. To the Socialists he replied that what they really feared was that ameliorative legislation might promote social contentment, and that their mills might in consequence have to stand still.

Provision for old age and incapacity remained to be made, and this likewise took the form of insurance. Before a bill on the subject was introduced, an outline of the intended proposals was submitted to the Prussian Economic Cabinet at the end of 1887, and later was published for general discussion. Criticisms and suggestions were invited from public authorities, associations of employers and workpeople, social workers, and the press, and only after this inquest of the thought of the nation had been made was a bill submitted in the Diet. Like the other two measures of social insurance, this likewise was compulsory, while the cost was equally divided between the workers and their employers, except that the state undertook to make a contribution to the pensions given. The bill was ultimately passed in May 1889, though by a small majority—185 against 165. The Conservatives and National Liberals voted solidly in its favor, but all the Clericals except thirteen, all the Radicals except one, and the whole of the Social Democrats voted against it.

The question of making provision for the unemployed, either in the form of insurance or assistance by work, was allowed to stand over, and meanwhile the municipal authorities were encouraged to regard this province of social providence as specially suited to local effort.

Of all the opposition offered to the social insurance laws that of the Socialists, the representatives of the class to be benefited, was the most incomprehensible. In later years the leaders of the party gave currency to the myth that they were the true friends of this beneficial legislation, and that without them it would not have come into existence. It is undoubtedly true that the Socialist agitation had directed public attention to social evils which had been ignored so long as they were borne by the victims patiently. Bismarck himself admitted that without that agitation social reform might have been indefinitely postponed. If, however, the Socialists entertained friendship for these laws, they showed it in remarkable ways. Most of their criticism was negative and barren, and their only positive action took the form of demands so extreme and impracticable that their effect, if not their purpose, was purely obstructive.

It was unfortunate that repression at this time went hand in hand with attempts to conciliate the working classes by ameliorative legislation, for the effect was to cause the government's professions of good-will to be received with sullen ingratitude. Hence as soon as social legislation was promised Bebel declared in the Diet (May 4, 1880), "To your positive measures for their benefit the workers reply with ringing laughter," while the Dresden party congress of 1882 formally decided to "reject state Socialism so long as it is inaugurated by Prince Bismarck and is designed to support the government system." The party soon had reason to change its mind, however, for the Copenhagen congress of 1883 decided to accept the proposed reforms for what they were worth. In later years it might truly be said that the blessings showered upon Bismarck's insurance legislation by the Social Democrats were more emphatic than their earlier curses; yet the fact remains that had the leaders of the party had their way the social insurance laws might not have been passed to the present day.

Edmond Vermeil

A STATE WITHOUT A POLITICAL IDEA

French historians have as a rule been critical of the dominant institutions of the German Empire. Edmond Vermeil was no exception. His several important works and years of teaching at the Sorbonne in Paris won him a name as a leading expert on Central Europe. What interested him most was not political or economic history in the traditional sense, but the temper and outlook which became common in modern Germany. He maintained that the spirit prevalent east of the Rhine was fundamentally unlike that of Western Europe, so that behind the superficial differences in policies and attitudes there was an essential difference of national character.

Considered from the point of view of its political structure, the Bismarckian Empire was what Guglielmo Ferrero called a "demo-monarchy." An evil-sounding term, but one which defined in a perfectly adequate manner the system which was developed in the German countries between 1815 and 1860, and which served as the framework of the Second Reich.

It is easy to see the curious compromise represented by German centralization when we set its resulting federal state *(Bundesstaat)* between the federation of states *(Staatenbund)* of the Germanic Confederation and the centralized state *(Einheitsstaat)* devised by the admirable Constitution of 1849, which never came into force in Germany. Bismarck vehemently opposed the constitutional ideal of 1848; but when, after 1850, he had accumulated valuable experience at the Diet of Frankfurt, the principal organ of the Germanic Confederation, he realized that Germany could not stop at a loose formula of federation. The original bond between Prussia and the Reich was the very thing to give him the desired solution. In order that Prussia might continue, as she wanted to at any cost, to exist as a "state" inside the Reich, it would be necessary to retain a certain federalism, that of the twenty-five Bismarckian states. But as it was no less indispensable to superimpose upon those states a strong central power armed with the required authority, that power was confided to that same Prussia, thanks to the personal union between Prussia

From Edmond Vermeil, *Germany's Three Reichs: Their History and Culture* (London, 1945), pp. 206–212. Reprinted by permission of Librairie Gallimard.

and the Reich. This combination was proposed by the Reichstag and accepted by Bismarck. The Prussian monarchy became imperial, in the Bismarckian sense of the term. The first minister of state of Prussia thus became chancellor of the empire.

This system, though certainly complicated, did not succeed badly. From 1871 to 1890, dynastic particularism did not offer Bismarck the opposition he seemed to fear. The successive rapid triumphs of centralization, on the other hand, inflicted a decisive defeat on the old federalism. Centralization had in its favor the majority of the political parties, and therefore the majority of the nation, which felt instinctively that the future belonged to the unification of German energies. National Liberals, who stood for the free circulation of goods and for economic centralization; Progressives who, faithful to the principles of 1848, sought political unity without on that account neglecting material unity; Social Democrats, who were interested in standardizing the condition of the workers in Germany—all these elements formed a large majority over the Prussian Conservatives, the Catholic Center, and the Democrats of the south, all more or less federalist.

As, on the other hand, the normal play of the constitution tended to aggrandize the legislation, the administration, and the competence of the Reich, the central power did not scruple to draw profit from these prerogatives, which could be extended at will. The process of unification carried out in Germany between 1871 and 1914 was of a striking character. But it is easily explained. A nation that arrived so late at this relative degree of political integration would try by every means to make up for lost time. All social classes, all organizations, all interests were drawn into this extraordinary whirlpool. Parliament legislated with feverish haste to satisfy the growing needs of the nation in its rapid advance.

Officially or tacitly the Reich, in extending its legislative competence, made rapid progress in the spheres in which it had the exclusive or the relative right to make laws, so that every legislative advance brought new means of control. It encroached even on those domains in which the states were supposed to be alone competent to legislate. Naturalization, the means of communication and transport, currency, the banking system, the civil code, all fell into its hands. On the administrative plane the sections of the vast imperial machine multiplied in consequence, with the formation of the immense army of officials of the Reich, the states, and the local authorities. The powers of the emperor and the chancellor increased similarly and supplanted those of the Federal Diet. The imperial offices, the germ of future ministries, were grouped around the chancellor, who tended to delegate a part of his responsibility to them. As for military unification, a great idea of Bismarck's, there was nothing in its way but the feeble obstacle of certain rights reserved to the states. Compulsory service was extended, and also served to unify the population of the Reich.

This craving for unification extended to the states themselves, which, to settle various questions, entered into conventions of military import in regard to railway rates and in regard to judiciary administration. Even the Federal Council, which favored these agreements, furthered the aims of centralization. While Prussian particularism tended to absorb the little particularisms of the country, the Reich integrated in itself all the particularisms at once. Federalism maintained its positions in the financial domain alone.

The states lost of necessity what the Reich gained. But this implied no danger to the future of the régime. The victory of centralization assured, in fact, that of Prussian hegemony. How would Bismarck's Germany have been able to develop without the permanent spread of Prussia's influence? Not that Prussia could govern the Reich as she liked. Still, no one in Germany could push Prussia in a particular direction or prevent her from acting as she pleased. Prussia applied to her rule the principles of Stein, fought against the preponderance of the bureaucracy, and tried to gain more elasticity and liberty through the play of administrative autonomy. She even sought to show as much consideration to the wishes of the toiling masses as to those of the aristocracy and the plutocracy. Bismarck was able to force the Junkers to make concessions. It was because Prussia, at once strong and supple, thus prepared herself with an eye on her mission that she was able to maintain a balance between federalism and centralization. The King of Prussia, as emperor, had control of the army and navy. The personal union and the prestige of the imperial function did not hurt Prussia, which could not be put into a subordinate position by centralization, having all the means of resistance.

Prussia, therefore, could not forgo leading Germany, though nothing constrained her to assume the leadership. Even when the central power developed considerably, she retained a large share of it, without effectively ruling the other states. Her hegemony amounted strictly to the total of the principles and institutions thanks to which she was impregnating the reconstituted nation with her juridical, administrative, and military spirit. The laws of the Reich had a Prussian aspect, and the German code was only a prolongation of the Prussian. The control the Reich exercised over the states was a control of the Prussian type. The fate of the states was indissolubly bound to that of Prussia as well as to that of the Reich. The Reich was, in fact, a "Prolonged Prussia." Prussia exercised a regulating influence. Not that there was a perfect organic liaison between her and Germany from the political and economic point of view. It was mainly the administration and the army that profited by the Prussian hegemony. By this method the former absolutism could be applied to the Second Reich under relatively modern forms.

There was nothing unnatural in this process, which seemed inevitable, since the empire was behind its neighbors. The strangeness began with the consequences of this unification on the political plane. The real threat to the régime was the play of political forces, the permanent conflict between Parliament and the government.

From 1815 to 1918, parliamentarism in Germany simply used its opportunities to work for unification. That was its distinctive feature, or, if preferred, the place it logically occupied in the Bismarckian system. Coupled with the centralization it favored, it proved to be a sort of mean between the system the Germanic Confederation had tried to introduce and the system sketched in the constitution of Frankfurt. It in no way excluded the rule of the crown and its personal servants. It left them all their executive authority. On the other hand, it entirely abandoned the sovereignty of the people in the Western sense of the term. It was the instrument of which the monarchy made use in order to find out what interests were at stake, to manipulate them, and to dominate them by setting them one against another. This amounts to saying that the Bismarckian Reich was a state without a political idea. That is why the Bismarckian institution of the Reichstag, which so surprised the Germans in 1867, is explained only by the history of German parliamentarism between 1815 and 1860. Bismarck, in fact, merely summed up and applied to the Reich the experience which had been gained by the forty states of the Germanic Confederation. And, as is known, the paths which German parliamentarism followed in this first period of its history show perfect regularity.

From 1860 to 1864, Prussian parliamentarism tried to seize power and to limit the rights of the crown. When Bismarck, prime minister of Prussia from 1862, intervened, he took the mean between the opposed tendencies, and prepared, thanks to three victorious wars, the solution of 1871.

We know that that solution, once it had arrived at maturity, provided on the one hand for a federal council which included the plenipotentiaries of the dynasties, which still retained a measure of sovereignty, and on the other hand for a monarch who was at the same time King of Prussia and Emperor, with a national Parliament or Reichstag superposed, as it were, on the Prussian "Landtag" and on the parliaments of the twenty-five states, and elected, like all the rest, by universal suffrage. If we add that it was the Reichstag itself that wanted to see the King of Prussia assume the imperial function, it will be understood that there was at an early stage a kind of solidarity between the two unitary organs, emperor and Reichstag, in face of the federal organ. What was then bound to come about, under Bismarck himself, was the substitution for that initial solidarity of a permanent conflict between the two central organs, particularly between Bismarck as chancellor and the parties represented in the Reichstag.

It was a strange delusion that Bismarck cherished from the beginning of this period. What he had feared above all was resistance from the dynasties. But the rapid unification and the very prosperity of the Reich, which were at once the condition and the consequence of unification, had the result not so much of producing federal difficulties as of giving new courage to the political parties and rendering them difficult to manage. Bismarck expected an always docile majority from a Parliament which he had organized as a simple state college and had deprived in advance of all authority of its own. This docile majority he never had. The imperial power, the Prussian power, and the secondary dynastic powers were all interested in agreeing together, in order to save for the old monarchism all that could be saved. But the parties and the Reichstag, swelled, as it were, from within by the progress of the Reich, stood in the way. The Federal Diet, whose meetings were secret and whose members were entirely out of touch with the people, effaced itself before the emperor and the chancellor as before the Reichstag. The very progress of centralization prevented the emperor, the chancellor, and the Diet from controlling the Reichstag.

The parliamentary institution saw its importance and its prestige continually growing through the very force of circumstances. The three years between elections had been converted into five. The Prussian Landtag (Diet) and the other parliaments vegetated in the shade. The collision became permanent between the chancellor, representative and creator of a monarchical absolutism mitigated by liberalism, and a Parliament indispensable for the work of legislation, but not sovereign. There was flagrant and irreconcilable strife between a power that was Prussian and monarchical in origin and spirit, and a people in which the conservative aristocracy, the big-business men, the middle classes, the proletariat, and the Catholic elements could not by themselves find the means of creating a new center of political crystallization. Prussia superimposed upon the Reich her legislation, administration, and army, in accordance with the method consecrated by the old territorial traditions. But the Reich, having grown too large, struggled wildly in the net and threatened to break it.

Undoubtedly the divisions between the parties permitted a chancellor as vigorous as Bismarck to govern after a fashion, all the more because foreign policy was entirely in his hands. But even in this sphere these divisions made things awkward for him. It is said that Bismarck invented "Realpolitik," a term used to veil the emptiness of German statecraft. And each party practiced "Realpolitik," even the Catholic Center. Each of them *socialized* itself, disciplined itself, and formed a compact block behind which the great trade-union organizations could be discerned. Bismarck fought the Center on the confessional plane, the budding Social Democracy on the social plane, the Conservatives and the National Liberals on the economic plane, the Progressives on the political plane. But these struggles made him the prisoner of his own creation. No law could be voted without the assent of the Reichstag. But Bismarck still imagined, as he had done in 1862 and in 1864, that legislation could be reconstructed by agreement, by compromise and collaboration between the crown and Parliament. Consequently, from 1871 to 1890, conflict between chancellor and Reichstag was continually breaking out. Bismarck even wondered, a little before his fall, whether the underground work of the parties would not destroy his constitution, and he was considering an antiparliamentary *coup d'état*. But it was he, and not the Reichstag, that quitted the political scene.

It was a tragic fall which, under the rule of William II, left the Reich without firm direction. On the one hand, the Reichstag was no more able to seize and organize power than it had been in the past. On the other hand, the imperial government lost In Bismarck Its surest defender and its best guarantor. The Germany of William II presented more and more, as the First World War approached, the spectacle of a nation which, though toiling with fervor, developing widely, and extending its positions throughout the world, was none the less *badly directed.*

The constitutional mechanisms no longer worked. The successors of Bismarck, the new emperor and his numerous chancellors, were neither the equals of their former master nor equal to events. How could they exercise with authority a power that Bismarck had cut to his own measure? As for the parliamentary institution, it was troubled, in Prussia and the Reich, by the critical problem of the franchise and of the real representation of the masses. How could it constitute a power capable of remedying the failings of the imperial monarchy? The Prussian franchise was antiquated, and the universal franchise of the Reich did not work properly. The more the central power extended its legislation, its administration, and its army, the more it seemed to be disabled in the face of the release of the energies and the magnitude of the interests represented by the Reichstag parties.

VI THE BISMARCKIAN LEGACY

Friedrich Meinecke

A SYNTHESIS OF POWER AND CULTURE

When Friedrich Meinecke embarked on his academic career, the great Leopold von Ranke was still writing his vast history of the world. When he died in 1954 at the patriarchal age of ninety-one, his fame was nearly equal to that of the great nineteenth-century master. The reputation he had won rested on a series of brilliant studies which sought to analyze the underlying ideas of modern political life. After the Second World War the grand old man of German historiography published his reflections on the tragic era in which he had lived, urging his nation to return to the humane ideals of its classic age.

In the Prussian state of Frederick William I and Frederick the Great there lived two souls, one capable of culture and the other hostile to culture. The Prussian army as created by Frederick William I brought forth a remarkably penetrating militarism that influenced all civil life and found its like in no neighboring state. However, as early as the travel sketches of Montesquieu, who lived in Hanoverian territory near the Prussian frontier, we find some unpleasant things about it. The question of the origin of Prussian militarism we can leave to one side; we wish to inquire here only into its influence on German destiny as a whole in the nineteenth century.

As long as the synthesis of intellect and power seemed to look hopeful in the nineteenth century, we regarded even militarism with a more benevolent eye; we emphasized the undoubtedly high moral qualities which were evident in it: the iron sense of duty, the ascetic strictness in service, the disciplining of the character in general. Easily overlooked, however, was the fact that this disciplining developed a leveling habit of conformity of mind which narrowed the vision and also often led to a thoughtless subserviency toward all higher authorities. This habit of conformity caused many of the richer springs of life to dry up. Furthermore, the advocates of Prussian militarism overlooked at first the fact that all sorts of unlovely practices and passions could rage under cover of exterior discipline.

Reprinted by permission of the publishers from Friedrich Meinecke, *The German Catastrophe: Reflections and Recollections,* trans. by Sidney Bradshaw Fay (Cambridge, Mass.: Harvard University Press, 1960), pp. 10–15.

Public life also might suffer from these effects of militarism if the statesmen and generals, who had grown comfortably important in the militarist atmosphere, had an influence on the life of the nation. This evil seemed apparent even at the time of the War of Liberation, when the synthesis of intellect and state was for the first time boldly attempted. The synthesis was in many ways brilliantly attested, but ultimately was fatally crippled by a militarily narrow-minded monarch and by an equally narrow-minded and at the same time egotistical caste of nobles and officers. The crippling of the reform movement, symbolized in 1819 by the dismissal of Wilhelm von Humboldt and Boyen, may be regarded as a victory in the Prussian state of the soul that was hostile to culture over the soul that was capable of culture. The rift ran straight through the whole nineteenth century and was inherited by the twentieth century. Finally, Prussian militarism also secured a large place for itself in the mixing pot into which Adolf Hitler threw together all substances and essences of German development which he found usable.

However, in the era when the empire was founded, the aspects of Prussian militarism which were bad and dangerous for the general well-being were obscured by the imposing proof of its power and discipline in its service for national unity and in the construction of Bismarck's empire. The military man now seemed to be a consecrated spirit—the lieutenant moved through the world as a young god and the civilian reserve lieutenant at least as a demigod. He had to rise to be reserve officer in order to exert his full influence in the upper-middle-class world and above all in the state administration. Thus militarism penetrated civilian life. Thus there developed a conventional Prussianism (*Borussismus*), a naive self-admiration in Prussian character, and together with it a serious narrowing of intellectual and political outlook. Everything was dissolved into a rigid conventionalism. One must have observed this type in countless examples with one's own eyes in the course of a long life, one must have felt it in one's own self, struggled with it, and gradually liberated one's self from it, in order to understand its power over men's minds—in order to understand finally the effect of the touching comedy in the Potsdam church on March 21, 1933, which Hitler played with Hindenburg beside the tomb of Frederick the Great. For here National Socialism was expected to appear as the heir and propagator of all the great and beautiful Prussian traditions.

A man like Theodore Fontane, whose lifework represents as none other all that was great and beautiful in the Prussian tradition, could, in a letter written in 1897, near the end of his life when he had grown critical and keen of insight, utter words of displeasure about the Prussian world around him. His testimony is not to be rejected simply because it is sharply exaggerated in every direction. "Borussism," he wrote, "is the lowest form of culture that has ever existed. Only Puritanism is still worse, because it is completely given to lying." And another time he wrote: "What must be crushed first of all is militarism."

This evil Borussism and militarism was like a heavy mortgage imposed on Bismarck's work and inherited from him by his hybrid successor, Hitler. There was, however, also something in the immediate contribution of Bismarck himself which lay on the border between good and evil and which in its further development was to expand more on the side of evil. The truth of this criticism would never be readily conceded by those who grew great under Bismarck's work and richly enjoyed its blessings. We Germans often felt so free and proud, in contrast with the whole previous German past, in this mightily flourishing empire of 1871 which gave living space to every one of us! But the staggering course of World War I and still more of World War II makes it impossible to pass over in silence the query whether the germs of the later evil were not really implanted in Bismarck's work from the outset. It is a query which courageous and unfettered historical thinking must pose in regard to every great and apparently beneficent historical phenomenon in which a degeneration takes place. One then breathes the atmosphere of the tragedy of history, of human and historical greatness, and also the problematical uncertainty which will ever hover around a Bismarck and his work—while Hitler's work must be reckoned as the eruption of the satanic principle in world history.

Consider now the year 1866 and Bismarck's blood and iron policy. Today we listen with more emotion to the voices which at that time expressed concern over the great evils of the future—voices of such important men as Jakob Burckhardt and Constantin Frantz, and one might add as a third the queer Swabian, Christian Planck. Bismarck's policy, according to them, was destroying certain foundations of Western culture and the community of states and was a really deep-reaching revolution which was opening the prospect of further revolutions and an era of wars. It meant, they said, the victory of Machiavellism over the principles of morality and justice in international relations and it let perish the finer and higher things of culture in a striving after power and pleasure.

Let us be honest. However one-sided these complaints may have been, there is a grain of truth in them. On the other hand, there are plenty of voices to defend Bismarck. They call attention to all the similar examples of Machiavellian practices in the rest of Europe of that day and especially to the fact that Bismarck himself recognized limits to his policy of force. These defenders likewise point out that in his peace policy after 1871 Bismarck did good service to the Western community of nations. "You know I cannot love Bismarck," a Danish historian friend said to me during the Third Reich, "but now I must say; Bismarck belongs to *our* world."

One must regard Bismarck as a borderline case. He still had in mind to some extent the conception of a synthesis of power and culture as it was understood by the leaders of the movement for German unity. These leaders themselves, with Treitschke at their head, originally were seriously offended by Bismarck's first steps in the period of the constitutional conflict, but became his defenders and admirers as a consequence of the war of 1866. The result was that in the synthesis of power and culture, of the things of the state and the things of the spirit, the preponderance slowly but steadily shifted further over to the side of power and its domain. From my own development I can bear witness to this—until, in the years before the First World War, a reaction of humanitarian feeling once more began to set in.

One can always object that the power-state and Machiavellism were not confined to Germany, that they were more often preached but not more strongly practiced by us Germans. This view is quite true. Specifically German, however, was the frankness and nakedness of the German power-state and Machiavellism, its hard and deliberate formulation as a principle of conduct, and the pleasure taken in its reckless consequences. Specifically German also was the tendency to elevate something primarily practical into a universal world-view theory. It was a serious thing for the future that these ideas about power-state and Machiavellism, at first expressed merely as theories, might become practical weapons in the hands of ruling authorities. The German power-state idea, whose history began with Hegel, was to find in Hitler its worst and most fatal application and extension.

The degeneration of the German people is what we are here trying, by groping and probing, to understand merely in its rough outlines. How difficult it is, however, to sketch a picture of the spiritual and cultural condition of Germany in the first decades after the founding of the empire in 1871, of the good as well as the bad germs in it! The judgment commonly expressed today, often merely parroting Nietzsche, that liberalism had become flat and shallow, settles nothing. The silver age of classical liberalism, of which we spoke, still persisted and still produced in art and science much that was brilliant, while the average level and everyday taste remained decidedly low. But no one then would have thought possible the emergence in educated Germany of a phenomenon like National Socialism—only the uneducated, proletarian Germany of Social Democracy was feared as a serious menace to our culture in the future. We, especially we younger Germans, felt exceedingly safe, entirely too safe, in the possession of a high national and cultural heritage.

Gerhard Ritter

THE LAST GREAT CABINET STATESMAN

The traditionalist school of German historians found a brilliant spokesman in Gerhard Ritter. A student of Hermann Oncken, he wrote prolifically on nearly every period of the history of Central Europe from the age of scholasticism to the resistance against Hitler in which he himself had participated. It was his

From Gerhard Ritter, *Europa und die Deutsche Frage: Betrachtungen über die geschichtliche Eigenart des deutschen Staatsdenkens* (Munich, 1948), pp. 77–86. Reprinted by permission of F. Bruckmann K.G. Verlag. Translated by Theodore S. Hamerow and William W. Beyer.

contention that the political institutions of Germany cannot be judged by the standards prevailing in Western Europe. They must be understood in the light of the unique historical experiences which have formed the outlook of the Germans. As for National Socialism, it was not the expression but an aberration of the national spirit. Germany today should reexamine the older, healthier tradition evident in the statecraft of the Junker from Schönhausen.

The liberal and democratic popular movement of 1848 had shown itself in practice powerless to create a new German national state against the opposition of the princely governments and the particularism of a large proportion of the German people. Not only armed force, but also the monarchical, conservative sentiment of sizable groups of the population, primarily though not exclusively in the eastern provinces of Prussia, had made the triumph of the reaction possible. The Habsburg state, hardly recovered from internal upheaval, had used threats of war reinforced by foreign alliances to undo the last, timid efforts of Prussia to save at least a part of the work of unification by peaceful agreement among the monarchical governments. Only under a particularly favorable constellation of the European powers could German nationalism risk a new attempt in this direction. For it had been demonstrated that Europe was not ready to accept the establishment of a new, large, national state in its midst without opposition. The danger of intervention by the great neighboring powers was all the more serious, because the Habsburg monarchy was obviously determined to reassert its old hegemony over Germany and to defend it in bloody conflict, if need be, against Prussian claims to leadership.

That is how the situation looked, and that is how Bismarck understood it. When at his first public appearance as minister he announced that he did not believe that the German problem could be solved in any way but through "blood and iron," he only meant to express this sober judgment, rejecting the visionary hopes of his liberal opponents that Prussia could achieve the leadership of a united Germany by a policy of "moral conquests," that is, by winning the support of public opinion. That he was essentially correct, in other words, that without an armed struggle against Austria the Prussian monarchy had practically no prospect of asserting its claim to leadership is at least highly probable, even if it naturally cannot be demonstrated beyond a doubt, no more than can any other of the so-called "historic necessities." European historical research has long been in fundamental agreement on this point. Particularly impressive is the recent work of a Swiss scholar who maintains that Bismarck's German policy was not a matter of personal choice, but was essentially dictated by true reason of state, that is, it represented an amazingly accurate estimate of the only way which could lead to his goal without excessive danger, given the nature of power relationships in Europe and in Germany. Bismarck's phrase about "blood and iron" belongs to those polished aphorisms which he used from time to time to describe a specific situation. They were intended as weapons, but when interpreted as general propositions, they gave rise to very many biased and erroneous opinions about him. On no account is the phrase to be understood as a declaration of a brutal and unscrupulous policy of war and conquest. He never pursued such a policy; indeed, he rejected it completely and unequivocally. But it is admittedly no accident that the phrase has such a shrill and harsh sound. There is a conscious and emphatic belligerence about it, and this belligerence was not without a demonic element.

The great biography of Bismarck by the Anglo-German historian Erich Eyck has recently illuminated this demonic element very sharply from the point of view of the older English liberalism associated with Gladstone. It concludes: "Rarely has nature endowed one man with greater riches. But she denied him a sense of right and justice." This verdict has been popularized and vulgarized by mass journalism to imply that for the greatest German statesman might came before right as a matter of principle, that he taught his Germans to share this view, and that he is therefore to be considered the forerunner and pathbreaker of Hitler. In the search for the "roots of National Socialism" in German history Bismarck thus usually appears in a very prominent position beside Frederick the Great, and the modification or destruction of the traditional respect for Bismarck by the German people seems to be one of the most urgent demands of that political reeducation to which our nation is now to be subjected.

No one will have to consider this problem more seriously than the practitioner of German historiography, which, we may venture to say, has been overshadowed for more than half a century by the spirit of Bismarck, which has allowed its political outlook to be largely determined by his ideas, which has with few exceptions believed in the infallibility of at least his foreign policy. As far as his influence in domestic affairs is concerned, there has always been much criticism, and the divisive effects of his activity as organizer and political educator have not gone unnoticed. But how much more profoundly than ever before has his entire lifework come to be questioned, now that the empire which he created has collapsed not only in its monarchical form as in 1918, but in its entirety, and as a result of a brutal policy of might which only too gladly invoked the traditions of Frederick the Great and Bismarck whenever it exalted the demands of power over justice and duty. In such circumstances it could be useful if our attention were directed by Eyck's book toward those aspects of the life of the great exponent of power politics which are particularly alarming to us today, but many of which were formerly overlooked. Among them are his highly biased view of all domestic policy as a constant struggle for power against the party system; the important role of personal hatred and personal ambition in that struggle; his ruthless, at times actually brutal disregard for individuals and legalities not only during the constitutional conflict in Prussia, but also in the period when he was imperial chancellor; his attachment to Junker social prejudices as well as his unmistakable streak of self-seeking; and the limitations in his understanding of domestic policy characteristic of the outlook prevalent east of the Elbe. But there are also instances when the passion of the diplomatic struggle seems to carry him beyond the usual restraints of reason of state, as in the unchivalrously harsh treatment of the city of Frankfurt in 1866, in the advocacy of bloody terror during the struggle against the French guerilla fighters and in the bombardment of Paris, or in the various attempts at intimidation in dealing with the young French Republic until 1875. What today seems to us most serious of all because of its lasting effect is the conscious abuse of political ideas and principles for purely tactical objectives, leading to the spiritual undermining of the great liberal movement which he first opposed and then tried to force into his service, until it degenerated into unprincipled opportunism. By treating the political idealism of the parties as pure doctrinairism, by attempting to transform the German parties of ideology into mere pressure groups, by pitting them against each other in order to assert the power and authority of his monarchical government over them, he destroyed a vast store of good will and a readiness for responsible collaboration, while intensifying economic, social, and religious antagonisms. By his autocratic conduct he also largely suppressed political self-reliance and the willingness to accept responsibility among his ministerial colleagues and among the highest officials of the empire. To speak of a political emasculation of the German middle class would probably be an exaggeration, but certainly after Bismarck's later years the bourgeoisie devoted itself more to economic than political problems. In contrast to Western Europe, parliamentary activity in our country offered to gifted, independent, and ambitious men little opportunity to attain effective power and public recognition. The result was the stagnation of political parties which came to be increasingly controlled by economic pressure groups, the apolitical Philistinism and uncritical loyalty of the petty bourgeois masses, a blind devotion to the state which could easily lead to a blunting of the sense of justice. The effect of Bismarck's rule on the conception of foreign policy accepted by the Germans will have to be discussed separately.

German historiography has no right to deny or prettify all these facts, especially since at times it too was infected with the spirit of "Realpolitik" understood in a Machiavellian sense, and preferred to depict with a certain aesthetic benevolence the demonic qualities in the character of its hero, at least to the extent that these qualities could be used to explain the genius of his political leadership. But there is something else which also belongs among the duties of truthfulness and justice. We must understand and judge each historical phenomenon according to the assumptions of its own time and environment. No political tradition is after all safe against the danger of deterioration. The "realism" of Bismarck is not necessarily refuted by the fact that it served later generations as a justification for deeds of violence. The historian who looks at Bismarck's political methods from English soil, through the eyes of his great opponent Gladstone, may too easily forget the difference of the soil on which he had to take his stand. While Gladstone was the classic, in a certain sense the most extreme champion of English insular and liberal statecraft, Bismarck was the most powerful and determined representative of a

Continental, hierarchically organized, actively belligerent great power. As a statesman he was closest to Richelieu. England's liberal empire, in full possession of its economic world hegemony and its naval supremacy, knew armed conflict only on the periphery of its existence, in certain overseas colonial areas. Its foreign policy could assume that all important conflicts of interest may be settled by agreement, by peaceful compromise and deliberation. Bismarck's Prussia was not so fortunate. Here, amid the Great Powers of the Continent, there was no possibility of "splendid isolation," of insular aloofness. In Germany all political hopes of the nation had to be realized through struggle. Instead of calm repose and conciliation, the indispensable virtue of a statesman was strict vigilance and the exertion of all energies. Bismarck himself justified the authoritarian government of his state, of the "constitutional monarchy," by the pressure of an international situation constantly threatened with struggles for power. He argued that the foreign policy of such a state could be successfully conducted only under the completely un-restrained sovereignty of a monarchical government independent of changing parliamentary majorities. German historiography has by and large agreed with him, seeing in his method of government a confirmation of Ranke's thesis concerning the primacy of foreign over domestic policy. According to this thesis the belligerent politics of the Continental state demand an inevitable sacrifice in civic free-dom, while the diplomatically more secure existence of the insular state or of the neutral small state makes possible a more easygoing, liberal form of government. Today we see clearly to what exaggera-tions this doctrine has led: as if the life of a Continental state were constantly threatened; as if there were not even on the Continent many opportunities for a peaceful compromise of conflicting inter-ests without constant resort to arms; as if there were not in a parliamentary state, as the example of France demonstrates, the possibility of a diplomacy which in the tenacious pursuit of power objectives, in its flexibility, in its capacity for swift decision is hardly hindered by parliamentary considerations. Yet it is nevertheless clear that for the great national states of the European continent the laws of life are different from those of the English insular world. Their internal structure as well as their conduct of foreign policy are determined by this difference. Even in England perceptive politicians have long recognized the fact. Philip Kerr, later Lord Lothian, wrote in November 1910 in the introduction to the first number of the journal of the Milner circle, *The Round Table:* "History has taught the Germans the bitter lesson that the citizen can be free only if the state to which he belongs is strong enough to guarantee his freedom."

It is above all from this point of view that Bismarck's war policy must be understood. It did not originate in the passions of a conqueror, adventurer, or militarist, but in the sober *raison d'état* of a military state. The Italian national state was also created only after a long series of armed conflicts, although there the moral authority of monarchical governments was much weaker than in Germany, while revolutionary zeal was much more ardent. Unlike Bismarck, moreover, the liberal statesman Cavour summoned the people against their princes, and enjoyed in addition the moral and military support of a leading foreign power. Even Switzerland and the United States of America did not achieve the development of their federal states into modern national states without major civil wars. The American war of secession of 1861–1865 actually revealed for the first time the horrors and cruelties of waging so-called total war, with its widespread destruction of the country and unprecedented human sacrifices. By comparison the campaign of three weeks which in 1866 decided the exclusion of Austria from the German Confederation seems almost a harmless military parade. It is thus not the conduct of the so-called wars of unification which tends to arouse the moral indignation of foreign observers, but rather their cold, calculated planning far in advance. Yet this is precisely the point at which the historic position of Bismarck in the whole of German and European history becomes most apparent.

He is, in a word, the last great cabinet statesman of European history, a belated Richelieu, to repeat the comparison. Better still, he is a spiritual descendant of Frederick the Great in a completely altered world. He is therefore a profoundly lonely figure, alien to his time. The European cabinets of the seventeenth and eighteenth century waged their wars in accordance with a sober calculation of the power interests of the state, in conscious contrast to the moral and religious passions which had been aroused during the age of religious wars and which had made warfare so bitter and cruel.

Bismarck conducted his wars in exactly this fashion, for reason of state pure and simple, in conscious rejection of that incitement of national passion without which no European since the French Revolution can any longer conceive a true war. For him war was in no sense a crusade either for the cause of God or of the nation, but simply a struggle of political forces to determine the superior power. He therefore needed neither the moral depreciation of his opponent nor any sort of self-glorification and self-righteousness. The simple realization that there were conflicting power interests which could no longer be reconciled in a peaceful way was enough. In this sense morality and politics were in his thought sharply separated from each other, whereas generally in the period since the French Revolution every political conflict tends toward "total" antagonism, that is, not only toward political hostility, but also toward the moral destruction of the opponent as an "enemy." For without such an arousal of feeling and passion a modern nation can no longer be led into war. What an artificial display of moral indignation and political conviction did the Western powers need in order to initiate the greatest cabinet war of the nineteenth century, the Crimean War against Russia. Even Bismarck could not outwardly dispense with it altogether, as the coming of the Franco-Prussian War shows. But in the Prussian monarchy the army was so strictly disciplined and so trained in apolitical loyalty to the throne, that he could undertake the "fratricidal war" of 1866 as a pure cabinet war, against the public opinion of all of Germany, even against the secret aversion of the Prussian chief of the general staff. And how free of moral resentment he himself was is clearly shown by his hard struggle with King William at the end of this cabinet war.

It should be thus quite apparent what a gulf separates Bismarck from a modern nationalist and adventurer like Adolf Hitler. Apart from the vast difference in their intellectual endowment and human quality, there is the distance separating two centuries of European history. Precisely that which characterizes the destroyer of Bismarck's empire and which is the real secret of his meteoric rise was completely alien to the founder of that empire: the fanaticism of national passion which depends upon the blind frenzy of the masses and knows so well how to arouse it. And precisely that which Hitler lacked completely, so that like a man possessed he staggered into the abyss and dragged his nation down with him, was the real secret of Bismarckian statecraft: sober, cool reason of state, unobscured by passion, imposing firm restraints on the exercise of power, pursued with the consummate skill of a born diplomat who knew the great courts of Europe as no other knew them. In view of this difference it is entirely unimportant that both men craved power as all active politicians do, that both were therefore inclined to equate their state with themselves. For the upstart this state was only a tool of the "party," in other words, his own tool. When the end came, the entire nation would and should go down with him. For the prime minister of old Prussia the possession of power was ultimately an opportunity to serve others.

Franz Schnabel

OLD MEANS AND OLD PURPOSES

When the reign of National Socialism finally came to an end amid the devastation of the Second World War, Gerhard Ritter and Franz Schnabel emerged as leaders of the postwar German historians. Whereas the former emphasized the continuing validity of national tradition, the latter became the spokesman for a cautious revisionism. Schnabel had established himself as a scholar of the first rank with the publication of his masterly history of Germany in the nineteenth century. But the Third Reich forced him into retirement from which he did not emerge until 1945, when he accepted the chair of modern history at the University of Munich. While recognizing Bismarck's great gifts, he criticized the nationalist solution of the unification problem.

We may correctly speak of Bismarck's being "misunderstood" nowadays in the sense that his work and activity have been viewed apart from their connection with the previous system of states and its political conceptions. Bismarck's conduct was dictated by a line

From Franz Schnabel, "The Bismarck Problem," in Hans Kohn, ed., *German History: Some New German Views* (Boston, 1954), pp. 82–89, 92–93. Reprinted by permission of the Beacon Press and George Allen & Unwin Ltd. Copyright © 1954 by the Beacon Press.

which traced back to Frederick the Great, Richelieu, Gustavus
Adolphus and Maurice de Saxe. They all contributed to the destruction of Western unity, to the establishment of sovereign states, and
to their mighty expansion by conquest, treaty-breaking and violence
against the weak. For a long time, Bismarck merely put modern
nationalism to his own uses. He was, first and foremost, the managing director of a state which played the role of a great power in
the European state system of five great powers and many smaller
powers; as yet, Prussia was not "saturated" within this state system.
Once he said that Prussia wore too heavy armor for her small body.
It is an image which corresponds to the old political thinking. Bismarck did not learn the new metaphors of nationalism. He was concerned with the interests of the state, with the state as a rational
system of analysis and action. Hence he remained strange to the
voluntarisms of the period of national states and democracy. The
program and slogans of nationalism—natural living space, historical
borders, assimilation and national will—which derived in part from
the French Revolution and for the rest from German romanticism,
were widespread among the liberals in the sixties and seventies, and
were already being fully acted upon among the Eastern European
peoples. Bismarck did not heed any of these slogans; he disregarded
this program. Even when he annexed Alsace and Lorraine, military
considerations were paramount in his mind. He belonged to the
system of states as it had been, when states looked out for themselves and wished to please only themselves, when the interests of
the state were all that was at stake and the interests of the people
were only of secondary concern. He brought two new great powers,
Prussia-Germany and Sardinia-Italy into the old European state system. As a result, he transformed the "European concert." The forces
which later put an axe to the entire historical state structure had
been in being for a long time, and Bismarck had to reckon with
them. But he still hoped to be able to bring them under control.

The methods used by Bismarck therefore derived from the old
policy of European governments. It saw in power the proper purpose
of the state. It had extricated the states from the medieval bonds of
universalism, and involved them in the struggle for hegemony or
balance of power. Modern nationalism was a new form of this spirit
of separatism. Therefore, Bismarck had been able to make it his

ally; with it he brought new elements of power into the battle array. He saw that, as a result, Europe would have to make rapid progress toward ruin. But he thought that the traditional state system, in whose categories he thought and acted, was strong. It would survive the profound contradiction which he brought about when he created a Prussian-German national state in Central Europe and at the same time tried to protect and preserve the pure dynastic states against the nationalities in Eastern Europe. For historical judgment this question is therefore clearly crucial: was there, in fact, any chance in Bismarck's time of giving up the free competition of interests? It would have made superfluous the old methods by which affairs had been conducted until then. Could there have been established as a consequence, cooperative life of men and peoples upon Christian principles, or at least a system corresponding to these principles more closely than the previous system? It cannot be maintained that Bismarck did not dare to set himself against his time. He thrust himself very energetically athwart the liberal and democratic movement, which certainly belonged to the advancing forces of the time, and hindered their development. On the other hand, the Frederician tradition in which he grew up was no longer a vital force at that instant; it regained its power during Bismarck's lifetime and mainly by his exertions. The choice was up to him. Would he remain under the spell of the old diplomacy and adopt in consequence its theory that the compact national state was the necessary form in which the nations could achieve their fulfillment? In that case, to be consistent, he would have had to "write off" the Habsburg monarchy. But he did not. Or, would he feel himself called upon to seek new paths in order to satisfy the nations of Central and Eastern European territories into a jumble of lands like the Balkans?

A statesman who did not accept the compact national state certainly had no lack of allies and forces at his disposal. Everywhere the majority of peoples still adhered to their hereditary princes. Of course, a small ducal state with a Serene Highness at its head no longer furnished an adequate area in which to function. But numerous connections had by then been set up between countries. Extension of the Prussian customs union (*Zollverein*) was possible; it was wholly justified by economic conditions, and only the school of the old diplomacy thwarted its achievement. Above all, however, the German Confederation could have been further developed. After the events of 1848 and 1849, the governments, including that of Prussia before Bismarck came upon the scene, were ready. Moreover, the question whether the vital rights of the nation could not be satisfied in this way as well, still remained completely open. The Danubian monarchy of the Habsburgs was not to be saved. It could break apart into national states. There would be frightful struggles especially in territories of mixed national composition. Or the Habsburg realms could be transformed into a Central European federation of nations, each living its own life again under new constitutional arrangements. In Vienna, as in Berlin, the decision had not yet been taken. Despite 1848–1849, the awakening of the nationalities in Eastern Europe had only begun. They took what they could use and were as yet not out of control. Only in the eighties did radicalism finally break through to them as a consequence of the system of 1866. There had been a time when national hatred between Englishmen and Scotsmen was elemental and fierce, yet it had been buried. To be sure, with the Irish this did not come successfully to pass. The examples of the United States and France were beyond contradiction. The nationalities were also set in motion by the doctrines of German romanticism. But after 1849 there was everywhere very great fear of Russia, and Pan-Slavism was still just something happening within literary romanticism. There was a profound basis in the course of modern history for the endeavor of all the peoples of Europe to develop, each in its own way, toward the goal of forming its own state. They were still in the habit of calling in a king from old dynasties, from foreign lands. Personal union was found to be a satisfactory solution, and there were many other such solutions. The demand for a compact national organism came only from a few parties, and was chiefly a product of the scholars. Furthermore, if a statesman knew world conditions, he could not help but see the problems of the Continent more profoundly than could Bismarck, whose policy was limited to the Continent. He could not escape the deep contradiction which cleaved apart the entire age: When nationalism had free course, it led to a dismemberment of Europe; at the same time, the technology of communications, which in the shape of the locomotive had already outrun the small states and was a pacemaker for the nation and for democracy, was advancing. It was overcoming distance ever more quickly and thereby compelling a changeover to world communications and a world economy.

There was, therefore, a good basis in the actual conditions for federal union of the Central and Eastern European peoples. The new arrangement could be developed upon an existing foundation with existing forces and energies. Any other goal signified an extension of the revolutionary policy which had already shaken Europe for so long a period of time. The revolutionary forces at various times had brought to the forefront one or another artificial power-state. These forces now included as well the active portion of the urban bourgeoisie which, as Ranke said at the time, dreamed that they could "construct out of their wits" their fatherland. Some constructed a *kleindeutsch* monarchy, others a *grossdeutsch* centralized republic. But the time when Bismarck was preparing and carrying through his work was also filled with plans tied to existing reality. Constantin Frantz was only the most active and the intellectually most important of those who told Bismarck that the security which the German people so urgently required when future world decisions would be made, could not be guaranteed by means of the isolated national state, and by the combination of alliances which Bismarck with great skill formed anew time and again. It should not be said, therefore, that the conceptions of a federative Europe were mere literature. The very *kleindeutsch* doctrine which came so conveniently to Bismarck's hand, had been elaborated in scholars' studies. And it is not correct either to say that the conception of a Central European federation of national states was premature, that it would only be justified when the nations would come to fear their own likeness unto God and saw themselves placed between two rising world powers. The moment quickly passed during which, as fate would have it, serious discussion of such a federation of Europe was possible. No one talked any more of union of the nations of Central and Eastern Europe, or of a Europe existing upon the basis of its own strength. Only in Bismarck's time could this idea have been carried out and the self-laceration of the nations prevented. It was already obvious that the appearance of Russia in Central

Europe, which anyone could see by 1849, was a world event of incalculable consequences. It necessarily opened up a new world epoch, with new methods in diplomacy and a new European attitude.

Here one may well object that no serious opponent of Bismarck, able to carry through such a policy, came forward. Controversial historiography, though it has its rights like any other, should never lose from view the fact that Germany at that time had lived for many centuries in political decrepitude. The German Confederation did indeed constitute a new beginning, but it was not yet a living political organism. Metternich, on whom rests responsibility for the three decades of German history from 1815 to 1848, permitted political life in the individual states to go farther. It was certainly of great value that the German people got the habit of acting in accordance with free political forms in the legislatures of south and central German states. But 1848 was the penalty paid because only those who supported the national state solutions had set programs. Austria's leadership in fact signified stagnation and reaction. Bismarck was the only statesman who took energetic action; he opened the valve to release the accumulated energies. An immense conflict in German life now broke out again, to be decided once and for all—on the one side the House of Habsburg, which for centuries had found its profit in maintaining things as they were; and on the other Frederician policy brought back to life! The liberals joined Bismarck's camp when he began to prove successful. The more they had previously placed their hopes upon Prussia and the Prussian monarchy, while rejecting Prussian methods, the longer was their resistance. The power of the personal factor in history was displayed with particular vigor in this regard. Yet the fact remains that the organization of Germany permitted of no delay, and that, in any event, whenever Austria would prove hesitant, Prussia would act.

Although Bismarck was therefore able to drive German history along the road to disaster, clearly he did not shoulder sole responsibility. It was borne equally by those other German forces still in existence at the time which did not set up a rival leader of equal stature. He was far superior to his liberal adversaries, like Roggenbach and Bennigsen, who wished to give a different constitution to the national state. One looks in vain in Prussia for a statesman of rank who would have been able to carry on the policy of peaceful dualism. In the middle-sized states there were no German princes as active on the *grossdeutsch,* federalist side as the Grand Duke of Baden was in the *kleindeutsch,* liberal camp; none was so popular as Duke Ernst of Gotha, the "sharpshooter Duke." Even Windthorst did not have his king's support; he was only an administrative minister and, when the hour of decision drew near, had once more been dropped from the ministry of state. In any case, we must look into the actual capacity of Count Beust as a statesman who, in the years of the foundation of the Reich, was Bismarck's leading opponent. Did he lose out to Bismarck because the Prussian statesman took a course of action which did not look far into the future, and so was much simpler and easier to follow? Because Bismarck opened the way for his policy, and followed it with no scruples of conscience, brushing aside violently considerations of law and justice? But it is still very doubtful whether the governing caste of the old Austrian monarchy would have permitted any statesman to carry through fundamental reorganization. It is true, of course, that Count Julius Andrassy, who was certainly a statesman of scope, received a free hand for a foreign policy which differed very greatly from that previously in effect. The nationalities brought forth personalities like Deák, who wished to guide nationalism along orderly channels. But, while Bismarck gave the example and brought on the decision, it was the Magyars who none the less were the essential driving force. The Czechs, on the contrary, hesitated for a while. At that time, there were important intellectuals among them. For a long time they endeavored to achieve peaceful reorganization of the monarchy, they kept in sight the danger threatening them from the east. But, for much too long, the answer which was given in Vienna, and in Berlin as well, was that things would not be changed under any circumstances. Archduke Franz Ferdinand came much too late. But it is often true in history that when the political turn of affairs is propitious, it brings forth the statesman who is needed. Who will deny that there were still many chances of development which even the Austrian court could not reject in the long run? It was Bismarck who destroyed these prospects. It may reasonably be doubted that, in the long run, such a federal state would have been able to provide security against the overwhelming growth of Russia. But the fact remains that there were forces in Central Europe which could have been spared and combined, which the rivalries and competition of the national state system used up at an enormous rate. Because of his origin and character, Bismarck was never able to take this path; in fact, as a result, he gave an intensely personal direction to the history of Germany and Europe. The situation which he faced at the start of his career was that the peoples of Europe were attacking the work of the Congress of Vienna; they wished once more to destroy it. But the decision was his that this would come about only by way of annexations and militarism, and that the nations had to adopt the capitalist system in self-preservation. Thus, very much against his will, he did most to bring about the dissolution of Central and Eastern Europe into purely independent national states.

We now know the steps by which this disaster, as we must call it today, was brought about. From the very first day of his official activity, Bismarck with fiery zeal loosened the ties with Austria, forced it out of Germany, abandoned it to the struggle of nationalities within it and created the Prussian-German state which could maintain itself only by alternating alliances with other power-states in the fashion of the old political system. The enormity of the enduring alliance with Russia against Austria was in itself a demonstration of the extent to which the new empire was totally incorporated into the great power system, entirely abandoned to the uncertain play of forces between the powers, and remaining wholly dependent upon one man's virtuosity. The many eulogists of Bismarck among German historians have praised to the highest his ostensible moderation in making the armistice with Austria at Nikolsburg in 1866; because it prevented the collapse of Austria at that moment, the later national radicalism of all nationalities found cause to regret it. In truth there is nothing in it either to be praised or blamed. The whole system of 1866, this last and much extolled "masterpiece" of the old style, resulted at once in the decline of the Habsburg Empire. Thus it was the cause of the isolation and downfall of the Bismarckian Empire as well. The nationalities were in fact encouraged by the success of the German movement. They took advantage of the weaknesses of the monarchy which had been defeated on the battlefield. As soon as the nationalities lay free and unprotected along the Russian border, Central Europe in turn could no longer maintain its own position. The old statecraft was utterly confounded. . . .

By destiny and tendency Bismarck's profession became the modern political system of reason of state and embattled interests. He found joy in this activity. He considered that territorial compactness and the independence of modern great states, which recognize legal order among themselves only In the shape of alternating alliances, constituted not merely a valuable, but in fact a final achievement of civilization. In order to safeguard and to extend this system of state power, he promoted the welfare of the people, though wholly in the spirit of the old statecraft, and was convinced that only a power-state could guarantee happiness and prosperity. Since the situation in which he found himself demanded his active intervention, he was not squeamish in the choice of his means and did not seek farther afield after new, better ways. He took for granted the state world in which he lived, and believed that Prussia was called upon to achieve something valuable in this system. He considered a compact state organism in the heart of Europe to be a higher form of life than a federation of states carried to another stage of development. There were many esteemed thinkers who, though they had their doubts, still sought to justify the statesman and to encourage him in this course. Powerful intellectual currents of the time assisted in this change. They led farther and farther away from the conception of law and from Christianity. But the statesman did not wholly realize what an alliance he was accepting. The life work which he built was certainly not profoundly thought out, but one would do injustice to Its master if one were to forget that the spiritual life of his time had in general lost all direction, that numerous and contradictory standpoints were represented with scholarship of equal breadth and with equal impressiveness, and that it was extremely difficult for the statesman to reach a position of fixity and validity. The creator of the second German Empire remained entirely gripped by the contradictions of his age. He made shift with the old means and the old purposes. This had never before led to enduring order; now the passions were all aroused as well. Bismarck took part in this release from control. He believed that he could utilize the new impulsion to be found in the crowd for the power of his state, and at the same time limit it by a rational system called reason of state. He did not come to a realization that in a world of such confusions there are tasks which go far beyond the state, and that it was becoming extremely necessary to bring the state back to its original purpose, to help establish the good, the right, the higher order. His position remained that the statesman's task consisted in nothing more than development of the state. Were there statesmen who saw farther than he? We cannot be sure. But he did become the first man of his time. Upon him depended essentially the further course of events. In history, however, only those forces are preserved which devote themselves to world historic goals. And the only standard by which peoples and civilizations can be measured and differentiated is whether a belief in a higher world order lives on in them.

G. P. Gooch
THE DIVORCE OF POLITICS FROM MORALS

George Peabody Gooch was blessed with that remarkable longevity which so many European historians seem to enjoy. He continued until his nineties to combine good scholarship with good writing as felicitously as ever. In the course of his long career he had proved himself a gifted lecturer and had sat in the House of Commons with the Liberals. But his claim to fame rests most securely on the numerous works of history published over more than half a century. While he was at home in many periods and many nations, his greatest interest was probably modern Germany. In his article on "Bismarck's Legacy" Gooch summarized a lifetime of study of the Iron Chancellor.

The lessons of Bismarck's political testament and unique career fall into two classes: those which concern statesmen of all times, and those specifically addressed to his own countrymen. The most important in the first category is enshrined in his celebrated aphorism: "Politics are the art of the possible," by which he meant the meticulous adjustment of ends to means. *Qui trop embrasse mal étreint.*

Reprinted in abridged form by permission of the publisher, from G. P. Gooch, "Bismarck's Legacy," *Foreign Affairs* 30 (1952): 527–530. Copyright © 1952 by the Council on Foreign Relations, Inc., New York.

Though nothing appears so obvious as the need for horse sense on the stony paths of *haute politique,* no maxim has proved more difficult to apply by those who scale the giddy summits of power. The difference between practicable aims and *Caesarenwahnsin* was sharply illustrated by the careers of Frederick the Great and Napoleon. The former staked his fortunes on the seizure of Silesia, which events were to prove within his capacity to accomplish and retain. Though he cherished and fulfilled other territorial ambitions, he never dreamed of fighting for them. Napoleon, on the other hand, intoxicated by his early victories in Italy, followed his delusive star and ended at St. Helena. The contrasted experiences of Bismarck and Hitler tell a similar tale. The former set out with a bold but limited resolve and when he reached his goal he sheathed the sword. It was not a case of the Prussian eagle borrowing the silky plumes of a dove, but a clear-eyed perception that there were limits to the strength of the Reich. Preventive wars he repudiated on the ground that no mortal could read the cards of Providence. The outstanding figure of the era of nationalism was neither an imperialist, for he never desired to impose German rule on alien races, nor a Pan-German, since he never aspired to bring all Germans into one fold. So long as he remained at the helm it could not be seriously argued that the new Reich had misused its strength. Hitler, on the other hand, neurotic, inexperienced, and trusting to his intuitions, was spurred forward by ambition as insatiable as that of Napoleon, and even before his appointment as chancellor he confided to Rauschning his fantastic dreams. Like Napoleon he never—in Byron's words —learned "that tempted fate will leave the loftiest star."

From this general principle of limiting risks stemmed a salutary exhortation to his countrymen, whose recurring temptation, located at the center of the European chessboard without natural frontiers, has been to hit out in all directions. During the medieval *Kaiserzeit* it was an urge to the south, in the twentieth century the call of East and West. A weak and divided Germany has always been a tempting bait to greedy neighbors, a united and powerful Germany a potential threat. Though Bismarck solemnly adjured her rulers to avoid the simultaneous estrangement of East and West, the warning was in vain. In that well-organized state, it has been remarked, there was anarchy at the top. While Tirpitz, bent on challenging Britain's naval predominance, urged the covering of the German flank through an understanding with Russia, Bethmann advocated friendly relations with England as a condition of forward moves in the Middle East. Both policies had their advantages and their risks, and a choice should have been made between them, but there was no Bismarck to make it. Had he revisited the scenes of his triumphs in the opening decade of the twentieth century, he would have been appalled by the transformation of a friendly England and a neutral Russia into potential foes. Had he returned for a second time at the close of the second decade, he would have pointed in grief and anger to the result of a policy of uninsurable risks. Like the Emperor Augustus after the defeat of Varus in the battle of the Teutoburger Wald, he might have murmured: "Give me back my legions."

Statesmen can learn much of their trade in Bismarck's school but not the whole. *Raison d'état* is a polite name for an ugly thing—the divorce of politics from morals. This gospel of anarchy, formulated though not invented by Machiavelli, has been practiced, if not always professed, by men of all races, all creeds, by good and bad alike. "If I see my opportunity," exclaimed Frederick the Great when the sudden death of the Emperor Charles VI opened the road to Breslau, "shall I not take it?" Napoleon dismissed as *idéologues* men who, as he believed, refused to look facts in the face. In the latter half of the nineteenth century Cavour and Bismarck played the familiar game with complete lack of moral scruple and with consummate skill. "If we did for ourselves what we do for our country," remarked the maker of United Italy, "what rascals we should be." Among the most successful of his stratagems was the dispatch of a beautiful countess to win the support of Napoleon III in expelling the Austrians from Lombardy. Though Bismarck stressed the importance of *imponderabilia,* when the right hour struck he acted and let the world say what it liked. It is an error to regard Prussia as more of an aggressor than Piedmont and Bismarck as morally inferior to Cavour. It was not till the shattering experience of the First World War revealed the insufficiency of the sovereign state in an increasingly interdependent world that Woodrow Wilson, General Smuts, Lord Cecil and other practical idealists launched a crusade for a system which seemed to promise less tragic results.

A second weakness in Bismarckian statesmanship was his neglect to train his countrymen for self-government. His grant of adult male suffrage suggested confidence in their wisdom and patriotism; but the Reichstag proved—and was intended to prove—little more than a fig-leaf, to use Liebknecht's drastic expression, to cover the nakedness of autocracy. That the power of the purse might have been put to better use is true enough, but the core of the constitution was the retention of final decisions in nonelective hands. A further bar to the democratization of Germany was the maintenance of the three-class voting system invented by Frederick William IV for Prussia, which contained two-thirds of the population of the Reich and in which the rapidly growing army of urban workers did not count. So obsessed was Bismarck by the principle of undivided responsibility that, though he was prepared to admit to office Bennigsen, the trusty leader of the National Liberals, he declined the request to bring two of his parliamentary colleagues with him, and the project of broadening the basis of government was dropped. When the Hohenzollern Empire fell with a crash in 1918 the problems of Weimar Germany had to be faced by amateurs.

It was not solely the fault of the chancellor, for there was little demand for parliamentary government except among the Socialists and the Radicals. Collaboration worked well enough in south Germany, but the emperor, the army chief, the Junkers and the great industrialists of the Rhineland objected to entrusting the proletariat with a substantial share of power. Conservative historians such as Hans Delbrück and Adalbert Wahl regarded the Bismarckian constitution as a model blending of popular representation with an irremovable executive, thus ensuring continuity in foreign policy and national defense. Liberal scholars, on the other hand, such as Ziekursch and Erich Eyck, censure him for ignoring the world-wide demand for parliamentary government. He could not live forever, and no other superman was in sight. Officials nominated or dominated by the ruler are as liable to make mistakes as ministers responsible to Parliament.

Bismarck bequeathed to his grateful countrymen a superb inheritance: a nation-state, a Triple Alliance to ensure its safety, a federal constitution which satisfied the rulers of the component states, the beginnings of social security, colonial territory, and a prestige unknown since the Emperor Barbarossa. Almost all these assets were thrown away by the shortsighted successors who forgot that politics are the art of the possible. It is one of the ironies of history that his most enduring monument should be a book which would never have been written but for the accident of his dismissal. The action of a young ruler, so hotly resented by his victim, unwittingly set the seal on his immeasurable renown.

Bismarck spoke disdainfully of "Professor Gladstone," but are the practitioners of Realpolitik as much wiser as they believe? Their weakness is to think too much of immediate returns and too little of the long-range results of their hammer strokes. Vast and splendid as was his intellect, he could see nothing and imagine nothing beyond the sovereign state pursuing exclusively its own supposed interests. Europe was only a geographical expression. The vision of an organized world, an international order resting on a willing partnership of self-governing national units, was beyond his ken. The presupposition of all profitable political and economic planning is a firm grasp of the unity of civilization. To the shaping of the human spirit for that supreme adventure of the human spirit he contributed nothing. He labored exclusively for his countrymen—first for Prussia and later for a Prussianized Reich—and was satisfied with their applause. In a word, he dates, for we have learned by bitter experience that nationalism is not enough. Yet the twentieth century will have little right to throw stones at the nineteenth until all the Great Powers begin to operate a system more conducive to human welfare than that which the Iron Chancellor practiced and preached.

Suggestions for Additional Reading

The historical literature on Bismarck is enormous. In Germany only Luther and Goethe have inspired a comparable volume of writing, while outside Central Europe no one can compete with the Iron Chancellor except Napoleon and Lincoln. An exhaustive list of books and articles dealing with his life and times has never been compiled. It is probably an impossible task. But the most comprehensive collection of titles appears in the standard bibliographical work on the history of Germany: F. C. Dahlmann and Georg Waitz, eds., *Quellenkunde der deutschen Geschichte*, 9th ed., 2 vols. (Leipzig, 1931), I: 870–897, 940–952. It cites well over two thousand publications. Works appearing in the last forty years are listed in the short but very useful book by Walter Bussmann, *Das Zeitalter Bismarcks* (Konstanz, 1956), pp. 251–274, which constitutes volume three, part two of Otto Brandt, Arnold Oskar Meyer and Leo Just, eds., *Handbuch der deutschen Geschichte*, 4 vols. (Marburg, Darmstadt, and Konstanz, 1952–1959). The sheer bulk of Bismarckian scholarship can be gauged from the fact that in Maximilian von Hagen, *Das Bismarckbild in der Literatur der Gegenwart* (Berlin, 1929), which describes the writings published in the twelve years from 1915 to 1927, there are accounts of more than a hundred and fifty works. And yet the author explains apologetically that he has been able to deal only with the more important titles.

While the German bibliographical publications are indispensable to the trained scholar, their effect on the beginner is unpredictable. It takes courage to face a list of hundreds of books in a foreign language, and it would perhaps be best if the neophyte did not expose himself right at the outset to what could prove an intimidating experience. There are fortunately several excellent accounts in English of the Bismarck literature. G. P. Gooch, "The Study of Bismarck," in his *Studies in German History* (London, 1948), pp. 300–341, is sure to stimulate the reader's interest. Scholarly, urbane, and perceptive, it is a model essay on bibliography. For a much briefer but still serviceable description see G. F. Howe, G. C. Boyce, T. R. S. Broughton et al., eds., *The American Historical Association's Guide to Historical Literature* (New York, 1961), pp. 555–557. Lawrence D. Steefel, who has written the standard work on the diplomacy of the Danish War of 1864, published an article on the Bismarckian literature of the 1920s entitled simply "Bismarck," *Journal of Modern History* 2 (1930): 74–95. For works published since the Second World War there are three useful critical reviews easily available to American readers. Andreas Dorpalen, "The German Historians and Bismarck," *Review of Politics* 15 (1953): 53–67, is the most comprehensive. As the title suggests, Hans Kohn, "Rethinking Recent German History," *ibid*. 14 (1952): 325–345, does not deal with the Bismarck problem exclusively, but it devotes a good deal of attention to the issues raised by the unification of Germany. Finally, Otto Pflanze in the early part of his article on "Bismarck and German Nationalism," *American Historical Review* 60 (1955): 548–566, describes recent interpretations of the Iron Chancellor.

The most important part of the Bismarck literature is what he himself wrote and said. The publication of his speeches and letters began while he was still alive, but there was no systematic collection of his various writings until the appearance of *Die gesammelten Werke* (15 vols. in 19, Berlin, 1924–1935). This great work of painstaking scholarship contains political polemics, conversations, addresses, letters, and memoirs. Yet despite its vast scope it is not complete, and should be supplemented with other compilations of Bismarck materials. For his speeches, for example, there is Horst Kohl, ed., *Die politischen Reden des Fürsten Bismarck*, 14 vols. (Stuttgart and Berlin, 1892–1905); for his diplomacy after the formation of the German Empire there are the first six volumes of Johannes Lepsius, Albrecht Mendelssohn Bartholdy, and Friedrich Thimme, eds., *Die grosse Politik der europäischen Kabinette, 1871–1914: Sammlung der diplomatischen Akten des Auswärtigen Amtes* (40 vols. in 54, Berlin, 1922–1927); and for his private talks there is Heinrich von Poschinger, *Fürst Bismarck und die Parlamentarier*, 3 vols. (Breslau, 1894–1896). Hans Rothfels has edited an excellent one-volume collection of his writings under the title *Otto von Bismarck: Deutscher Staat* (Munich, 1925), which constitutes volume twenty-one of the series *Der deutsche Staatsgedanke*. The introduction to this book, by the way, provides a thoughtful analysis of its protagonist's political philosophy.

While it would be futile to attempt serious research in the Bismarckian period without a good reading knowledge of German, the amount of material available in English is not inconsiderable. The memoirs were translated under the title *Bismarck: The Man and the Statesman*, 2 vols. (New York and London, 1899); some of the diplomatic writings from *Die grosse Politik* appear in the first volume of E. T. S. Dugdale, ed., *German Diplomatic Documents, 1871–1914*, 4 vols. (London, 1928–1931); the three solid volumes of the *Tischgespräche* have been reduced to one in Charles Lowe, ed., *Bismarck's Table Talk* (London, 1895); and some of the important collections of letters were published as *The Correspondence of William I and Bismarck*, 2 vols. (New York, 1903), and *The Love Letters of Bismarck* (New York and London, 1901). The American reader can thus obtain in his native language a firsthand acquaintance with the Iron Chancellor.

Next in importance to Bismarck's public and private papers are the writings of those who worked with him during his thirty years as the leading statesman of Germany. The vast literature of reminiscences, however, must be handled with care. The number of people who met the Iron Chancellor in one capacity or another was huge, and many of them were eager to bask in the reflected glory of his name. Moritz Busch, Bismarck's propagandist and confidant, published his diary in an English translation immediately after the statesman's death under the title *Bismarck: Some Secret Pages of His History*, 2 vols. (New York, 1898). The German edition in a somewhat censored form appeared a year later as *Tagebuchblätter*, 3 vols. (Leipzig, 1899). Robert Lucius von Ballhausen was a prominent politician and minister of agriculture in the later years of the reign of William I. His *Bismarck-Erinnerungen* (Stuttgart, 1920) presents an impressive and detailed portrait of the chancellor. Robert von Keudell knew the Bismarck family intimately, so that his *Fürst und Fürstin Bismarck: Erinnerungen aus den Jahren 1846–1872* (Berlin and Stuttgart, 1901) is a revealing account of the private life as well as the political activity of its hero during the struggle for national unification. Some of the most valuable memoirs were written by officials whose task it was to execute the chancellor's diplomatic designs. The diaries of Prince Chlodwig zu Hohenlohe-Schillingsfürst, *Denkwürdigkeiten*, 2 vols. (Stuttgart and Leipzig, 1906), are of major significance. They have appeared in English as *Memoirs of Prince Chlodwig of Hohenlohe-Schillingsfuerst*, 2 vols. (New York, 1906). General Hans Lothar von Schweinitz, who served under Bismarck as his country's ambassador to Austria and Russia, made important disclosures about the statecraft of his chief in *Denkwürdigkeiten des Botschafters General v. Schweinitz*, 2 vols. (Berlin, 1927). And Count Alfred von Waldersee in his recollections edited by H. O. Meisner as *Denkwürdigkeiten des General-Feldmarschalls Alfred Grafen von Waldersee*, 3 vols. (Stuttgart and Berlin, 1922–1923) throws light on the Iron Chancellor's last years in power.

The biographies of Bismarck continue to multiply, as both critics and defenders reinterpret his career in the light of subsequent history. Selections from Erich Marcks, A. J. P. Taylor, Otto Pflanze, Erich Eyck, and C. Grant Robertson appear in this book. But there are several other lives of the Iron Chancellor which ought not to be overlooked. Max Lenz, *Geschichte Bismarck* (Leipzig, 1902) is one of the earliest biographical studies, but it can still be read with profit. For the period of the constitutional conflict and the wars of unification there is the account in English by James Wycliffe Headlam, *Bismarck and the Foundation of the German Empire* (New York, 1899). The best French biography remains Paul Matter, *Bismarck et son temps,* 3 vols. (Paris, 1905–1908). Written before the First World War, these works accepted the state which Bismarck had created as viable and sound. Then came the collapse of the German Empire, which produced a revisionist school of Bismarckian scholarship. Such adverse interpretations as Karl Scheffler, *Bismarck: Eine Studie* (Leipzig, 1919), Hermann Kantorowicz, *Bismarcks Schatten* (Freiburg, 1921), and Friedrich Wilhelm Foerster, *Bismarcks Werk im Licht der föderalistischen Kritik* (Ludwigsburg, 1921), contended that the Iron Chancellor was ultimately responsible for the tragedy which had befallen his country, since the ends as well as the means of his diplomacy were bound to lead to disaster. The argument, however, failed to persuade many readers. The prevailing view was expressed in Otto Hammann, *Der missverstandne Bismarck: Zwanzig Jahre deutscher Weltpolitik* (Berlin, 1921), which maintained that it was not Bismarck but his inept successors who must bear the blame for Germany's ruin. Only since the Second World War has there been among scholars a consistently critical attitude toward Bismarck, although he still has his champions in historians like Arnold Oskar Meyer, *Bismarck: Der Mensch und der Staatsmann* (Stuttgart, 1949), and the more restrained Wilhelm Mommsen, *Bismarck: Ein politisches Lebensbild* (Munich, 1959).

An understanding of Bismarck's life necessarily depends on an understanding of his time. The activities of the statesman must be seen in their proper milieu, so that a study of political and economic history ought to supplement the reading of biographical accounts. On the rise of the movement for national unification in Germany from the War of Liberation to the Franco-Prussian War there is still the substantial opus of Adolphus William Ward, *Germany, 1815–1890,* 3 vols.

(Cambridge, 1916–1918). It is largely overshadowed, however, by two other major works which are no less scholarly and much more penetrating: Erich Brandenburg, *Die Reichsgründung,* 2 vols. (Leipzig, 1916), and Erich Marcks, *Der Aufstieg des Reiches: Deutsche Geschichte von 1807–1871/78,* 2 vols. (Stuttgart, 1936). Both agree that the ultimate objectives of Bismarckian statecraft were not only sound but necessary. For the German Empire William Harbutt Dawson holds up surprisingly well. But his book is no substitute for the volumes of Johannes Ziekursch and Adalbert Wahl. The former's history, openly critical of the chancellor's autocratic tendencies, is probably the best over-all treatment of the period. Yet on many points it should be checked with the latter's *Deutsche Geschichte von der Reichsgründung bis zum Ausbruch des Weltkriegs (1871 bis 1914),* 4 vols. (Stuttgart, 1926–1936), a spirited defense of Bismarck's political philosophy written from a conservative point of view. While German historians have generally avoided any out-and-out condemnation of the unifier of their country, foreign scholars have felt no similar reticence. The Englishman A. J. P. Taylor, *The Course of German History* (New York, 1946), the American Koppel S. Pinson, *Modern Germany* (New York, 1954), and the Frenchman Edmond Vermeil, *L'Allemangne: Essai d'explication* (Paris, 1940), translated as *Germany's Three Reichs* (London, 1945), agree that the Iron Chancellor taught his countrymen to worship power and submit to authority. This is also the conclusion reached more recently by Hajo Holborn in his massive *History of Modern Germany,* 3 vols. (New York, 1959–1969).